JavaScript Unleashed *Build Interactive Web Apps with Ease*

A Complete Guide to Mastering JavaScript and Web Development

MIGUEL FARMER

RAFEAL SANDERS

Table of Content

TABLE OF CONTENTS

INTRODUCTION

Welcome to **"JavaScript Unleashed: Build Interactive Web Apps with Ease – A Complete Guide to Mastering JavaScript and Web Development."** This book is designed to take you on an exciting and comprehensive journey through the world of web development, focusing on the power and versatility of JavaScript. Whether you're a beginner looking to dive into the fundamentals of web development or an experienced developer aiming to sharpen your JavaScript skills, this guide will equip you with the knowledge and practical tools to build robust, dynamic, and interactive web applications.

In today's fast-paced digital world, **JavaScript** stands as the backbone of modern web development. It's the language that powers the interactive elements of websites, from simple animations to complex single-page applications (SPAs). With its ever-expanding ecosystem and the constant rise of new frameworks and libraries, JavaScript has become one of the most crucial technologies in the development of both client-side and server-side web applications.

In this book, we break down JavaScript from the ground up, covering everything from the very basics of syntax to advanced concepts such as **asynchronous programming**, **JavaScript frameworks** like **React.js** and **Vue.js**, and **Progressive Web Apps (PWAs)**. As you progress, you'll build real-world projects, gaining hands-on experience and an in-depth understanding of how to use JavaScript effectively to create high-performance, user-friendly web applications.

What You'll Learn in This Book

1. **JavaScript Fundamentals**:
   - We'll start with the basics—understanding the syntax, variables, functions, and data structures. These are the building blocks upon which all your future JavaScript skills will rest. By the end of this section, you will be comfortable with the core concepts of JavaScript, ready to take on more advanced topics.

2. **Advanced JavaScript Topics**:
   - Once you've mastered the basics, we'll dive into more complex concepts such as **closures**, **higher-order functions**, and **prototypal inheritance**. You will also learn

how to effectively handle asynchronous code with **callbacks**, **promises**, and **async/await**.

3. **Working with the DOM**:

   o **The Document Object Model (DOM)** is the interface between your JavaScript code and the HTML structure of your web pages. We'll explore how to manipulate the DOM to dynamically update content, handle events, and create a seamless user experience.

4. **Building Web Applications**:

   o This book takes you beyond just JavaScript and introduces you to building complete web applications. You'll learn about **API integration**, **state management**, and using **databases** with **Node.js**. You will also learn the intricacies of creating **Progressive Web Apps (PWAs)** that work offline and feel like native apps.

5. **Frontend Frameworks**:

   o JavaScript is at the heart of many popular frameworks like **React**, **Vue.js**, and **Angular**. You'll get a solid introduction to these frameworks and learn how to use them to build scalable, maintainable applications.

These frameworks are essential for creating modern web apps and provide powerful tools for working with state, components, and routing.

6. **Backend Development with Node.js and Express**:
   - JavaScript isn't limited to the frontend; it's also a powerful language for backend development. We'll explore **Node.js**, a runtime that allows you to run JavaScript on the server side, and **Express.js**, a minimal web framework for creating RESTful APIs. You will also learn how to connect your JavaScript app to databases, such as **MongoDB** and **SQL databases**, making your web apps dynamic and data-driven.

7. **Security Best Practices**:
   - Security is paramount in web development. We will explore best practices to **secure your JavaScript applications**, protect them from common vulnerabilities like **XSS** (Cross-Site Scripting) and **CSRF** (Cross-Site Request Forgery), and make your app safe for users.

8. **Deployment and Performance Optimization**:

o Building a great web app isn't enough if it doesn't perform well or is difficult to deploy. This book will guide you through **deploying** your web apps to popular platforms like **Netlify**, **Heroku**, and **Vercel**, as well as show you techniques for **optimizing JavaScript performance** to ensure your app runs efficiently, even under heavy load.

Why This Book?

In the constantly evolving world of web development, JavaScript remains the most important language for creating interactive and user-friendly web experiences. However, despite its power, JavaScript can be overwhelming for beginners, and even experienced developers often struggle with best practices, performance optimization, and staying up to date with the latest features and frameworks.

This book has been crafted to address those challenges. Each chapter builds on the previous one, gradually increasing in complexity and equipping you with the tools and techniques you need to become a proficient web developer. We take a **hands-on approach**, providing real-world examples and building actual projects along the way. This practical experience will help you internalize core concepts and best practices, enabling you to apply your skills to real-world scenarios.

Additionally, we've avoided jargon and overly complex explanations. The content is written in a conversational style, making it easy to follow and understand, regardless of your current level of expertise. We focus on **clarity** and **relevance**, ensuring that you don't just learn the theory but also how to apply it in a real-world context.

Who Should Read This Book?

- **Beginners** who want to learn JavaScript from scratch and understand its importance in modern web development.
- **Intermediate developers** who want to sharpen their JavaScript skills, deepen their understanding, and explore advanced concepts such as asynchronous programming, service workers, and modern frameworks.
- **Frontend developers** who want to broaden their skillset and gain proficiency in backend technologies like Node.js, Express.js, and full-stack development.

- **Anyone** who wants to build fast, interactive, and scalable web applications using the latest JavaScript technologies and practices.

How to Use This Book

You can approach this book in two ways:

1. **Start from the beginning** if you're new to JavaScript and want to follow the natural progression of learning the language.
2. **Jump to specific chapters** if you're an experienced developer looking to refresh or deepen your knowledge in certain areas, such as React.js, Node.js, or security best practices.

What's Next?

By the end of this book, you'll be equipped to build sophisticated, interactive, and secure web applications from start to finish. You'll have hands-on experience with everything from basic JavaScript to full-stack development, and you'll understand the latest best practices in both frontend and backend development.

Whether you want to work as a **frontend developer**, **backend developer**, or **full-stack developer**, mastering JavaScript and the tools in this book will open doors to numerous opportunities in the tech world. You'll also be ready to keep up with future advancements in the JavaScript ecosystem and contribute to modern web development projects confidently.

CHAPTER 1

INTRODUCTION TO JAVASCRIPT AND WEB DEVELOPMENT

Why JavaScript is Essential for Modern Web Apps

JavaScript is at the heart of modern web development. It is a versatile programming language that enables developers to create dynamic, interactive, and feature-rich websites. In the past, websites were static, consisting mainly of HTML and CSS. However, with the rise of JavaScript, web development evolved significantly, allowing websites to respond to user interactions, manipulate data in real-time, and even update content without refreshing the entire page. This ability to create a seamless, interactive user experience is why JavaScript has become indispensable for web development.

Here are some reasons why JavaScript is essential for modern web apps:

- **Interactivity**: JavaScript enables features like forms, slideshows, real-time content updates, and animations, making websites interactive.
- **Cross-Platform Compatibility**: JavaScript runs on all major browsers, making it the go-to language for client-

15

side development. Its versatility extends to both front-end (user interface) and back-end (server-side) development through technologies like Node.js.

- **Wide Adoption**: Nearly all websites use JavaScript, making it a fundamental skill for any web developer.

Key Concepts: Browsers, the DOM, and JavaScript Engines

To understand JavaScript's role in web development, it's important to get familiar with a few key concepts:

- **Browsers**: Browsers are software programs that allow users to view and interact with web pages. Popular browsers include Google Chrome, Mozilla Firefox, Safari, and Microsoft Edge. Browsers interpret HTML, CSS, and JavaScript to display web content.
- **The DOM (Document Object Model)**: The DOM is an interface that allows JavaScript to interact with the content of a web page. It represents the structure of a web page as a tree-like model, where each element (HTML tag) is a "node." JavaScript can manipulate the DOM by adding, deleting, or modifying elements, styles, and attributes dynamically. This is what makes JavaScript essential for creating interactive web applications.
- **JavaScript Engines**: A JavaScript engine is a program that executes JavaScript code. Every browser has its own engine to interpret and run JavaScript. For instance:

    o   Google Chrome uses the V8 engine.

    o   Firefox uses SpiderMonkey.

    o   Safari uses JavaScriptCore (Nitro).

These engines parse the JavaScript code, compile it into machine code, and then execute it, allowing the web page to be interactive.

How JavaScript Fits into Front-End and Back-End Development

JavaScript plays a crucial role in both front-end and back-end development:

- **Front-End Development (Client-Side)**: JavaScript is most commonly used in front-end development to build dynamic user interfaces (UIs). With the help of JavaScript, developers can create interactive elements like buttons, forms, sliders, pop-ups, and live content updates without requiring a page reload. Libraries and frameworks like React.js, Angular, and Vue.js simplify and streamline front-end development.

- **Back-End Development (Server-Side)**: JavaScript is also used in back-end development through **Node.js**. Node.js is a runtime environment that allows developers to write server-side code in JavaScript. This means that developers can use JavaScript for both client-side and server-side tasks, streamlining the development process

17

and making it easier to maintain a full-stack JavaScript application. Node.js is popular for building scalable network applications and APIs.

Real-World Example: A Simple "Hello World" Web Page

Let's start with the classic "Hello World" example, which will help you understand how JavaScript works in the browser. Below is a basic example of a web page that displays a greeting when the user clicks a button:

html

```html
<!DOCTYPE html>
<html lang="en">
<head>
    <meta charset="UTF-8">
    <meta name="viewport" content="width=device-width, initial-scale=1.0">
    <title>Simple JavaScript Example</title>
</head>
<body>
    <h1>Welcome to JavaScript!</h1>
    <button id="helloButton">Click me!</button>

    <script>
        // JavaScript to handle button click event
```

18

```
        const            button             =
document.getElementById("helloButton");

        button.addEventListener("click",
function() {
            alert("Hello, World! You've clicked
the button.");
        });
    </script>
</body>
</html>
```

Explanation of the Example:

- **HTML Structure**: The page includes a header (`<h1>`) and a button (`<button>`). The button has an `id` attribute that uniquely identifies it.

- **JavaScript**: The `<script>` tag contains JavaScript code. This code finds the button using `document.getElementById("helloButton")`, and adds an event listener. When the button is clicked, the browser will display an alert saying "Hello, World!".

- **DOM Manipulation**: By using JavaScript to interact with the DOM, we make the web page interactive. This is a fundamental use of JavaScript in web development.

What's Next?

Now that we've covered the basics of JavaScript and its role in modern web development, you should have a solid understanding of how JavaScript fits into web apps and its importance. From here, we will dive deeper into how you can start building more complex web apps, manipulating the DOM, and utilizing JavaScript to bring your web projects to life.

In the next chapters, we'll start exploring variables, data types, functions, and control flow in JavaScript. These fundamental concepts are crucial as you build more advanced features in your web apps.

This chapter sets the stage for diving deeper into JavaScript by providing context for why it's such a powerful tool for web development and introducing some key technical concepts with an easy-to-understand example. As you progress through the book, we'll continue breaking down complex topics into manageable sections, ensuring both beginners and experts can follow along.

CHAPTER 2

SETTING UP YOUR DEVELOPMENT ENVIRONMENT

Before you dive deep into JavaScript programming, it's important to set up your development environment properly. The right tools and practices will ensure a smooth development process, whether you're writing code, debugging, or collaborating on projects. This chapter covers the essential tools for writing JavaScript, debugging with browser developer tools, introducing version control with Git, and setting up your first development environment for a JavaScript project.

Tools for Writing JavaScript: IDEs, Text Editors, and Debugging Tools

A well-organized development environment is essential for writing, testing, and maintaining JavaScript code efficiently. Here are the primary tools you'll need:

IDEs (Integrated Development Environments)

IDEs are full-featured software applications that provide tools for writing, testing, and debugging code. They typically include

21

features like syntax highlighting, code completion, error detection, and built-in terminal access. For JavaScript development, some popular IDEs include:

1. **Visual Studio Code (VS Code)**
   - **Why Use It**: VS Code is one of the most popular IDEs for JavaScript development. It's lightweight, fast, and extensible, with a vast collection of extensions available. It supports features like IntelliSense (code completion), Git integration, built-in terminal, and debugging tools.
   - **Best For**: Beginners to advanced developers, as it supports a wide range of programming languages and tools.
   - **How to Use**: Download from VS Code's website. Once installed, you can add JavaScript extensions for linting, debugging, and Git support.

2. **WebStorm**
   - **Why Use It**: WebStorm is a powerful IDE designed specifically for JavaScript and web development. It provides excellent code navigation, intelligent code completion, and powerful debugging features.
   - **Best For**: Developers working on larger, more complex web applications who prefer a full-fledged IDE with all features built-in.

22

- o **How to Use**: You can get WebStorm from JetBrains' website, but it requires a paid license after a trial period.

Text Editors

Text editors are simpler than IDEs but still very powerful. They allow you to write and edit code quickly and efficiently. Some popular text editors include:

1. **Sublime Text**
   - o **Why Use It**: Sublime Text is fast, lightweight, and highly customizable. It has robust support for syntax highlighting and plugins.
   - o **Best For**: Developers who need a simple, yet powerful editor with a minimalistic interface.
   - o **How to Use**: Download Sublime from their website, then install plugins for JavaScript support as needed.

2. **Atom**
   - o **Why Use It**: Atom is a free, open-source text editor built by GitHub. It's highly customizable and has a large community of contributors.
   - o **Best For**: Developers who prefer a customizable experience with an easy-to-use interface.

- o **How to Use**: Download Atom from GitHub, then install packages like `ide-java` or `atom-ide-ui` for JavaScript development.

Debugging Tools

Debugging tools help identify and fix errors in your JavaScript code. There are a few key tools you'll rely on for effective debugging:

1. **Browser Developer Tools** (Chrome DevTools, Firefox Developer Tools, etc.)
   - o Every modern browser (Chrome, Firefox, Safari) comes with built-in developer tools that allow you to inspect, debug, and test your JavaScript code in real-time.
   - o **Key Features**: Console, debugger, network request tracking, and performance monitoring.
   - o **Best For**: Real-time debugging, testing DOM manipulations, inspecting network requests, and viewing console logs.

How to Use Browser Developer Tools for Real-Time Debugging

Browser developer tools are an essential part of any JavaScript developer's toolkit. Here's how to get started:

1. **Opening Developer Tools**

   o In **Google Chrome**, press F12 or right-click anywhere on a page and choose "Inspect" to open DevTools.

   o In **Firefox**, press F12 or right-click and select "Inspect Element."

   o In **Safari**, go to "Develop" in the top menu and select "Show Web Inspector."

2. **Console Tab**:

   o Use the **Console** tab to log JavaScript output and debug your code. You can print variables, check errors, and test snippets of JavaScript.

   o Example: To log a variable, simply type `console.log(variableName)` in your JavaScript code, and the output will appear in the console.

3. **Debugger Tab**:

   o The **Debugger** tab lets you set breakpoints in your JavaScript code. This allows you to pause execution of your code at a specific point, inspect variables, and step through your code line-by-line to troubleshoot problems.

   o To set a breakpoint, open the **Sources** tab, navigate to your script, and click on the line number where you want the execution to pause.

4. **Network Tab**:

- o The **Network** tab tracks HTTP requests made by your JavaScript code, such as AJAX calls or fetch requests. This is invaluable for debugging issues with data retrieval.
- o You can inspect request headers, responses, and status codes to make sure your app is communicating with APIs correctly.

Introduction to Version Control with Git

Version control systems like Git are crucial for managing your project's codebase and collaborating with other developers. Git helps you track changes, revert to previous versions, and share your code with others efficiently.

1. **What is Git?**
   - o Git is a distributed version control system that keeps track of changes made to files and allows you to collaborate with others. Each developer has a local of the codebase and can make changes independently, syncing with the central repository when needed.
2. **Setting Up Git**
   - o Install Git from the official website.
   - o Set up your Git configuration by running:

```
arduino
```

```
git config --global user.name "Your
Name"
git config --global user.email
"youremail@example.com"
```

3. **Git Workflow**

   o **Clone**: To start working on a project, first clone the repository with:

   ```
   bash
   ```

   ```
   git clone <repository_url>
   ```

   o **Commit**: After making changes, stage them using `git add .` and commit with:

   ```
   sql
   ```

   ```
   git commit -m "Commit message
   describing changes"
   ```

   o **Push**: Once you're happy with your changes, push them to the remote repository:

   ```
   css
   ```

   ```
   git push origin main
   ```

27

4. **GitHub**

- o For online collaboration and sharing your code, you can use platforms like **GitHub**. GitHub provides remote repositories where you can store your code and collaborate with others.

Example: Setting Up Your First Development Environment for a Project

Let's walk through setting up your first development environment for a simple JavaScript project:

1. **Create a Project Folder**

   - o Create a new folder on your computer called `my-first-project`.

2. **Set Up Git**

   - o Navigate to the `my-first-project` folder and initialize a new Git repository:

     ```csharp
     git init
     ```

3. **Create Your HTML and JavaScript Files**

   - o Inside the project folder, create an `index.html` file and a `script.js` file.
   - o In `index.html`, add basic HTML structure:

```
html
```

```
<!DOCTYPE html>
<html lang="en">
<head>
    <meta charset="UTF-8">
    <meta           name="viewport"
content="width=device-width,
initial-scale=1.0">
    <title>My First Project</title>
</head>
<body>
    <h1>Hello, JavaScript!</h1>
    <button      id="clickMe">Click
me</button>
    <script
src="script.js"></script>
</body>
</html>
```

o   In `script.js`, add JavaScript:

```
javascript
```

```
document.getElementById("clickMe").
addEventListener("click", function()
{
    alert("Hello, World!");
});
```

4. **Run the Project**

   o   Open `index.html` in your browser. Click the button, and you should see the alert "Hello, World!" pop up.

5. **Track Your Changes with Git**

   o   Add the files to the Git staging area:

```
csharp

git add .
```

   o   Commit your changes:

```
sql

git commit -m "Initial commit with HTML and JavaScript"
```

Now, you've set up a basic JavaScript project and tracked the changes using Git. You can continue building on this foundation as you learn more about JavaScript development.

Conclusion

This chapter introduced you to essential tools for writing JavaScript, including IDEs, text editors, and browser debugging tools. It also provided an overview of version control with Git, allowing you to track changes and collaborate on projects. With your development environment set up, you are ready to dive deeper into JavaScript and build interactive web apps with ease.

CHAPTER 3

FUNDAMENTALS OF JAVASCRIPT SYNTAX

In this chapter, we will cover the foundational aspects of JavaScript syntax. Understanding variables, data types, operators, functions, and control flow is essential to becoming proficient in JavaScript. These concepts form the core building blocks of JavaScript programming and will help you write clean, maintainable code.

Variables, Data Types, and Basic Operators

Variables

A **variable** is used to store data that can be referenced and manipulated in a program. In JavaScript, we declare variables using one of three keywords:

- `var`: The traditional way of declaring variables, but it has some issues with scoping.
- `let`: The modern and preferred way of declaring variables, offering block-scoping.

- **const**: Used to declare constants, which cannot be reassigned after they are initialized.

javascript

```
let age = 25;    // Declaring a variable using let
const name = "Alice";    // Declaring a constant
```

Data Types

JavaScript has several built-in data types:

- **Primitive Types**:
  - **String**: Text data.

    javascript

    ```
    let greeting = "Hello, World!";
    ```

  - **Number**: Integer or floating-point numbers.

    javascript

    ```
    let score = 100;
    let temperature = 36.5;
    ```

  - **Boolean**: Represents true or false.

    javascript

    ```
    let isJavaScriptFun = true;
    ```

○ **Undefined**: Represents a variable that hasn't been assigned a value.

```javascript
let unassignedVar;
console.log(unassignedVar);        //
undefined
```

○ **Null**: Represents an intentional absence of value.

```javascript
let emptyValue = null;
```

- **Non-Primitive Types (Objects)**: Objects, arrays, and functions.

  ○ **Object**: A collection of key-value pairs.

```javascript
let person = {
    name: "John",
    age: 30
};
```

Basic Operators

JavaScript supports several types of operators for performing operations on variables and values:

- **Arithmetic Operators**: Used to perform mathematical calculations.

javascript

```
let sum = 5 + 3;      // Addition: 8
let difference = 5 - 3;    // Subtraction:
2
let product = 5 * 3;    // Multiplication:
15
let quotient = 5 / 3;    // Division: 1.6667
```

- **Comparison Operators**: Used to compare values and return boolean results.

javascript

```
let isEqual = (5 == 3);    // false
let isGreaterThan = (5 > 3);    // true
```

- **Logical Operators**: Used to combine multiple conditions.

javascript

```
let isAdult = true;
let isStudent = false;
let result = isAdult && isStudent;    //
false (both conditions must be true)
```

Functions and Scope

Functions

A **function** is a block of reusable code that performs a specific task. Functions allow us to avoid redundancy and keep our code organized.

- **Function Declaration**: A function can be declared with the `function` keyword.

    javascript

    ```javascript
    function greet(name) {
        console.log("Hello, " + name + "!");
    }
    greet("Alice");    //    Outputs:    "Hello,
    Alice!"
    ```

- **Function Expression**: Functions can also be assigned to variables.

    javascript

    ```javascript
    const sayGoodbye = function(name) {
        console.log("Goodbye, " + name + "!");
    };
    sayGoodbye("Bob");    // Outputs: "Goodbye,
    Bob!"
    ```

- **Arrow Functions**: A more concise syntax for writing functions, introduced in ES6.

javascript

```
const add = (a, b) => a + b;
console.log(add(2, 3));  // Outputs: 5
```

Scope

Scope refers to the context in which a variable is accessible. JavaScript has two main types of scope:

- **Global Scope**: Variables declared outside of any function or block are in the global scope.
- **Local Scope**: Variables declared within a function or block are only accessible within that function or block.

Example:

javascript

```
let globalVar = "I'm a global variable!";

function testScope() {
    let localVar = "I'm a local variable!";
    console.log(globalVar);  // Accessible
    console.log(localVar);   // Accessible
}
```

```
console.log(globalVar);    // Accessible
console.log(localVar);     // Error: localVar is
not defined
```

Control Flow (if-else, switch)

Control flow statements determine the order in which code is executed based on conditions.

if-else Statements

The `if` statement is used to execute code based on a condition. If the condition is true, the code inside the block runs; otherwise, it doesn't.

javascript

```
let age = 20;
if (age >= 18) {
    console.log("You are an adult.");
} else {
    console.log("You are a minor.");
}
```

switch Statement

The `switch` statement is a cleaner alternative to multiple `if-else` conditions when comparing the same variable to different values.

```javascript
let fruit = "apple";

switch (fruit) {
    case "apple":
        console.log("It's an apple.");
        break;
    case "banana":
        console.log("It's a banana.");
        break;
    default:
        console.log("Unknown fruit.");
}
```

Real-World Example: Creating a Simple Number Guessing Game

Let's put these fundamentals together by building a **number guessing game**. The program will ask the user to guess a number between 1 and 10 and provide feedback on whether the guess is too high, too low, or correct.

```html
<!DOCTYPE html>
<html lang="en">
<head>
    <meta charset="UTF-8">
```

39

```html
    <meta name="viewport" content="width=device-
width, initial-scale=1.0">
    <title>Number Guessing Game</title>
</head>
<body>
    <h1>Guess the Number!</h1>
    <p>Guess a number between 1 and 10:</p>
    <input type="number" id="guess" />
    <button         onclick="checkGuess()">Check
Guess</button>
    <p id="feedback"></p>

    <script>
        // Generate a random number between 1 and
10
        const         secretNumber         =
Math.floor(Math.random() * 10) + 1;

        // Function to check the user's guess
        function checkGuess() {
            let             guess             =
document.getElementById("guess").value;
            let          feedback          =
document.getElementById("feedback");

            // Validate the input
            if (guess < 1 || guess > 10 ||
isNaN(guess)) {
```

40

```
        feedback.textContent  =  "Please
enter a number between 1 and 10.";
            return;
        }


        // Check if the guess is correct, too
high, or too low
        if (guess == secretNumber) {
            feedback.textContent          =
"Congratulations!  You  guessed  the  correct
number!";
        } else if (guess < secretNumber) {
            feedback.textContent = "Too low!
Try again.";
        } else {
            feedback.textContent  =   "Too
high! Try again.";
        }
    }
  </script>
</body>
</html>
```

Explanation of the Game:

- **Variables**: We define `secretNumber` to store the randomly generated number between 1 and 10.

41

- **Functions**: The `checkGuess()` function is called when the user clicks the button. It compares the user's guess with the `secretNumber` and gives feedback.
- **Control Flow**: The `if-else` statement checks whether the user's guess is correct, too high, or too low.

Conclusion

In this chapter, we covered the essential fundamentals of JavaScript syntax:

- **Variables** and their types, including primitive and non-primitive data types.
- **Basic operators** for performing arithmetic, comparison, and logical operations.
- **Functions** for organizing code and **scope** to understand where variables can be accessed.
- **Control flow** with `if-else` and `switch` statements for decision-making.

By the end of this chapter, you've built your first interactive game—a number guessing game! In the next chapter, we will explore more advanced concepts, like working with arrays and objects in JavaScript.

CHAPTER 4

WORKING WITH ARRAYS AND OBJECTS

In this chapter, we will dive into two of the most essential and commonly used data structures in JavaScript: **Arrays** and **Objects**. These structures allow you to store and organize multiple values efficiently. Additionally, we'll explore the methods you can use to manipulate these structures and iterate through them using loops like `for`, `forEach`, and `map`. By the end of this chapter, you'll understand how to work with arrays and objects to build more complex applications.

Understanding Arrays, Objects, and Their Methods

Arrays

An **array** is an ordered collection of values. You can store multiple values of any data type in an array, including strings, numbers, booleans, or even other arrays and objects.

Creating Arrays:

```
javascript
```

```javascript
let numbers = [1, 2, 3, 4, 5];   // Array of
numbers
let fruits = ["apple", "banana", "cherry"];   //
Array of strings
let mixed = [1, "apple", true, null];   // Array
with different data types
```

Accessing Array Elements: You can access an array element using its index (remember that JavaScript arrays are zero-indexed):

```
javascript
```

```javascript
let firstFruit = fruits[0]; // "apple"
let secondNumber = numbers[1]; // 2
```

Common Array Methods:

- **push()**: Adds an element to the end of the array.

  ```
  javascript
  ```

  ```javascript
  fruits.push("orange");
  console.log(fruits);        //        ["apple",
  "banana", "cherry", "orange"]
  ```

- **pop()**: Removes the last element from the array.

  ```
  javascript
  ```

44

```
fruits.pop();
console.log(fruits);      //      ["apple",
"banana", "cherry"]
```

- **shift()**: Removes the first element from the array.

```javascript
fruits.shift();
console.log(fruits);      //      ["banana",
"cherry"]
```

- **unshift()**: Adds an element to the beginning of the array.

```javascript
fruits.unshift("kiwi");
console.log(fruits); // ["kiwi", "banana",
"cherry"]
```

- **slice()**: Returns a shallow of a portion of an array.

```javascript
let slicedFruits = fruits.slice(1, 3);
console.log(slicedFruits);   //   ["banana",
"cherry"]
```

Objects

An **object** is an unordered collection of key-value pairs. The keys (or properties) can be strings or symbols, and the values can be any data type, including other objects or arrays.

Creating Objects:

javascript

```
let person = {
    name: "Alice",
    age: 30,
    isEmployed: true
};
```

Accessing Object Properties: You can access an object's properties using either dot notation or bracket notation:

javascript

```
let name = person.name; // "Alice"
let age = person["age"]; // 30
```

Adding and Modifying Object Properties:

javascript

```
person.job = "Engineer";    // Adding a new
property
```

46

```
person.age  =  31;    //  Modifying  an  existing
property
```

Common Object Methods:

- **Object.keys()**: Returns an array of an object's keys.

  javascript

  ```
  console.log(Object.keys(person));      //
  ["name", "age", "isEmployed", "job"]
  ```

- **Object.values()**: Returns an array of an object's values.

  javascript

  ```
  console.log(Object.values(person));    //
  ["Alice", 31, true, "Engineer"]
  ```

- **Object.entries()**: Returns an array of key-value pairs.

  javascript

  ```
  console.log(Object.entries(person));    //
  [["name",      "Alice"],      ["age",      31],
  ["isEmployed", true], ["job", "Engineer"]]
  ```

How to Loop Through Data Using `for`, `forEach`, *and* `map`

To work with arrays and objects in real-world applications, you often need to iterate over them. There are several ways to loop through data in JavaScript.

`for` Loop:

The `for` loop is the most traditional way to iterate over arrays. It provides full control over the loop counter and iteration.

```
javascript
```

```javascript
let fruits = ["apple", "banana", "cherry"];
for (let i = 0; i < fruits.length; i++) {
    console.log(fruits[i]);
}
```

Output:

```
nginx
```

```
apple
banana
cherry
```

`forEach()` Method:

The `forEach()` method is a cleaner way to loop through an array. It automatically passes each element in the array to a callback function.

`javascript`

```
let fruits = ["apple", "banana", "cherry"];
fruits.forEach(function(fruit) {
    console.log(fruit);
});
```

Output:

`nginx`

```
apple
banana
cherry
```

The `forEach()` method is especially useful for operations that don't require returning a result.

`map()` Method:

The `map()` method creates a new array populated with the results of calling a provided function on every element in the calling array. It's commonly used when you need to transform data in an array.

```javascript
let numbers = [1, 2, 3, 4];
let             squaredNumbers             =
numbers.map(function(number) {
    return number * number;
});
console.log(squaredNumbers); // [1, 4, 9, 16]
```

Real-World Example: Building a To-Do List App with Arrays and Objects

Let's put all these concepts together by building a simple **to-do list app**. This will demonstrate how you can work with arrays and objects to create a useful, interactive feature.

Here's a simple JavaScript-based to-do list app:

```html
<!DOCTYPE html>
<html lang="en">
<head>
    <meta charset="UTF-8">
```

```html
    <meta name="viewport" content="width=device-
width, initial-scale=1.0">
    <title>To-Do List</title>
</head>
<body>
    <h1>My To-Do List</h1>
    <input          type="text"         id="newTodo"
placeholder="Add a new task">
    <button onclick="addTodo()">Add</button>
    <ul id="todoList"></ul>

    <script>
        let todos = [
            {    task:    "Learn    JavaScript",
completed: false },
            { task: "Build a website", completed:
false }
        ];

        // Function to display the to-do list
        function displayTodos() {
            const          todoList          =
document.getElementById("todoList");
            todoList.innerHTML = "";  // Clear
current list

            todos.forEach(function(todo,   index)
{
```

```
            let           li           =
document.createElement("li");
            li.textContent = todo.task;

            // Toggle completed status on
click
            li.addEventListener("click",
function() {
              todo.completed              =
!todo.completed;
              li.style.textDecoration     =
todo.completed ? "line-through" : "none";
            });

            todoList.appendChild(li);
        });
    }

    // Function to add a new task
    function addTodo() {
        const      newTodoInput       =
document.getElementById("newTodo");
        const         newTask         =
newTodoInput.value.trim();

        if (newTask) {
            todos.push({   task:   newTask,
completed: false });
```

```
                newTodoInput.value   =   "";   //
Clear input field
                displayTodos();  //  Update  the
list
        }
    }


    // Initial display of to-do list
    displayTodos();
</script>
</body>
</html>
```

Explanation of the To-Do List App:

- **Array of Objects**: The `todos` array contains objects, where each object represents a to-do item with two properties: `task` (the description of the task) and `completed` (a boolean to track whether the task is done).
- **forEach()**: The `forEach()` method is used to loop through the `todos` array and display each item on the page.
- **click Event**: When you click a to-do item, the `completed` property toggles between `true` and `false`. This changes the appearance of the item (strikes through the text if completed).

53

- **Adding New Todos**: The `addTodo()` function allows you to add a new task to the `todos` array by typing it into the input field and clicking the "Add" button.

Key Concepts in This Example:

- **Arrays**: We use an array to store our to-do items.
- **Objects**: Each to-do item is represented by an object with `task` and `completed` properties.
- **Methods**: We use `forEach()` to loop through the array and manipulate DOM elements based on user interaction.
- **Event Handling**: We attach a `click` event listener to each to-do item to toggle its completion status.

Conclusion

In this chapter, we learned how to work with **arrays** and **objects**, two of the most important data structures in JavaScript. We explored how to manipulate arrays using built-in methods like `push()`, `pop()`, and `map()`. We also learned how to work with objects, accessing their properties and using methods like `Object.keys()`.

We applied these concepts to build a simple to-do list app, which showcases how arrays and objects can be used to store and manage data in a real-world application.

In the next chapter, we'll dive into more advanced JavaScript concepts, such as asynchronous programming with promises and async/await.

CHAPTER 5

FUNCTIONS IN DEPTH

Functions are fundamental building blocks in JavaScript, enabling code to be organized, reusable, and maintainable. In this chapter, we'll explore advanced concepts related to functions, such as **function declarations vs. expressions**, **arrow functions**, **higher-order functions**, and **closures**. Additionally, we'll dive into the special **this keyword**, which behaves differently in various contexts. To wrap up, we'll apply these concepts to build a **reusable calculator module** to demonstrate their practical use.

Function Declarations vs. Expressions

In JavaScript, functions can be defined in two primary ways: **function declarations** and **function expressions**. While both allow you to define a function, their behavior and usage are slightly different.

Function Declarations

A **function declaration** is the traditional way to define a function. It uses the `function` keyword, followed by the function name, parentheses (for parameters), and curly braces (for the body of the function).

```
javascript

function add(a, b) {
    return a + b;
}

console.log(add(5, 3)); // Outputs: 8
```

Key Characteristics:

- **Hoisting**: Function declarations are **hoisted**. This means they can be called before they are defined in the code. The entire function definition is moved to the top during the execution phase.

Function Expressions

A **function expression** defines a function and assigns it to a variable. This function can be anonymous (without a name) or named.

```
javascript

const subtract = function(a, b) {
    return a - b;
};

console.log(subtract(10, 4)); // Outputs: 6
```

Key Characteristics:

- **No Hoisting**: Unlike function declarations, function expressions are **not hoisted**. You can only call the function after it is defined.
- **Anonymous Functions**: Function expressions can be anonymous (no name).

javascript

```
const multiply = function(a, b) {
    return a * b;
};
```

Arrow Functions and Higher-Order Functions

Arrow Functions

Arrow functions, introduced in ES6, provide a more concise syntax for writing functions. They are especially useful for shorter functions or callback functions.

javascript

```
const divide = (a, b) => a / b;

console.log(divide(10, 2)); // Outputs: 5
```

Key Characteristics:

- **Concise Syntax**: Arrow functions eliminate the need for the `function` keyword and curly braces when the function body has a single expression.
- **Implicit Return**: If the function consists of only one expression, it will implicitly return the result of that expression without the need for a `return` statement.

With Multiple Statements: If the function body has multiple statements, curly braces are needed, and you must explicitly use `return` to output a value.

```javascript
const greet = (name) => {
    console.log("Hello, " + name);
    return "Greetings!";
};
```

Higher-Order Functions

A **higher-order function** is a function that can accept one or more functions as arguments, return a function, or both. These functions are powerful tools for functional programming and allow for greater abstraction.

```javascript
// Example of a higher-order function:
function applyOperation(a, b, operation) {
```

```
    return operation(a, b);
}


const sum = applyOperation(5, 3, (x, y) => x +
y);
console.log(sum); // Outputs: 8
```

Key Characteristics:

- **Functions as Arguments**: Higher-order functions can accept other functions as arguments (like the `operation` function in the example).
- **Returning Functions**: Higher-order functions can also return functions.

```
javascript


const multiplier = (factor) => (x) => x * factor;
const double = multiplier(2);
console.log(double(4)); // Outputs: 8
```

Closures and the `this` Keyword

Closures

A **closure** is a function that "remembers" its lexical scope even when the function is executed outside that scope. This means that the inner function retains access to variables from its outer function, even after the outer function has finished executing.

```javascript

function outer() {
    let count = 0;
    return function inner() {
        count++;
        console.log(count);
    };
}

const increment = outer();  // inner() has access
to count
increment();  // Outputs: 1
increment();  // Outputs: 2
```

Key Characteristics:

- **Encapsulation**: Closures help create private variables that are not directly accessible from outside the function but can be modified or accessed via the closure.
- **Memory Efficiency**: Closures allow you to retain the state across function calls without needing global variables.

The this Keyword

The **this** keyword refers to the context in which a function is called. Its value depends on how the function is invoked.

In Global Context: In a regular function, when called globally, `this` refers to the global object (`window` in browsers).

javascript

```
function showThis() {
    console.log(this);  // In browsers, this
refers to the global object (window)
}
showThis();
```

In Object Methods: When `this` is used inside a method of an object, it refers to the object itself.

javascript

```
const person = {
    name: "Alice",
    greet: function() {
        console.log("Hello, " + this.name);
    }
};
person.greet(); // Outputs: Hello, Alice
```

In Arrow Functions: Arrow functions do not have their own `this`. They inherit `this` from the surrounding (lexical) context, which can be useful for avoiding some common pitfalls with regular functions.

62

```
javascript

const person = {
    name: "Bob",
    greet: () => {
        console.log("Hello, " + this.name);   //
`this` refers to the global object (not the
person object)
    }
};
person.greet(); // Outputs: Hello, undefined
```

Real-World Example: Creating a Reusable Calculator Module

Now let's put all these concepts together by creating a **reusable calculator module** using functions, closures, and the `this` keyword.

```
javascript

const Calculator = function() {
    let result = 0;

    // Function to perform addition
    this.add = function(x) {
        result += x;
        return result;
    };
```

```javascript
// Function to perform subtraction
this.subtract = function(x) {
    result -= x;
    return result;
};


// Function to perform multiplication
this.multiply = function(x) {
    result *= x;
    return result;
};


// Function to perform division
this.divide = function(x) {
    if (x === 0) {
        console.log("Cannot    divide    by
zero!");
        return result;
    }
    result /= x;
    return result;
};


// Function to reset the calculator
this.reset = function() {
    result = 0;
    return result;
};
```

```javascript
    // Function to get the current result
    this.getResult = function() {
        return result;
    };
};

// Create a new calculator instance
const calc = new Calculator();

console.log(calc.add(5)); // Outputs: 5
console.log(calc.multiply(2)); // Outputs: 10
console.log(calc.subtract(3)); // Outputs: 7
console.log(calc.divide(7)); // Outputs: 1
console.log(calc.reset()); // Outputs: 0
console.log(calc.getResult()); // Outputs: 0
```

Explanation of the Calculator Module:

- **Object-Oriented Approach**: The calculator is encapsulated in a constructor function, `Calculator`, which initializes a private `result` variable using closures.

- **Methods**: Functions like `add()`, `subtract()`, `multiply()`, and `divide()` manipulate the `result` and return the updated value. Each method is bound to the calculator object (`this`), allowing for chaining and reuse.

- **Encapsulation**: The internal `result` variable is kept private, and can only be accessed or modified through the provided methods, ensuring that the calculator's state is managed safely.

Conclusion

In this chapter, we explored advanced JavaScript functions concepts:

- **Function declarations vs. expressions**: We learned the difference between how functions are defined and invoked.
- **Arrow functions**: We simplified function syntax and discussed the `this` keyword in the context of arrow functions.
- **Higher-order functions**: We saw how functions can take other functions as arguments or return functions, enabling powerful patterns like functional composition.
- **Closures**: We explored how closures allow functions to "remember" their surrounding context, making it possible to encapsulate state.
- **`this` keyword**: We examined how `this` behaves differently in various contexts, including global scope, object methods, and arrow functions.

Finally, we applied these concepts by creating a reusable calculator module, which can be extended and customized for more complex applications.

In the next chapter, we will dive into **asynchronous JavaScript** to learn how to handle asynchronous operations like API calls and file handling effectively.

CHAPTER 6

JAVASCRIPT ASYNCHRONOUS PROGRAMMING

Asynchronous programming is a key concept in JavaScript that allows for the handling of tasks that take time, such as fetching data from a server or waiting for a user to click a button, without blocking the main thread of execution. In this chapter, we'll explore **callback functions**, **promises**, and **async/await**, and discuss how to manage asynchronous operations effectively. We'll also apply these concepts in a real-world example of fetching data from an API and displaying it dynamically on a web page.

Callback Functions, Promises, and Async/Await

Callback Functions

A **callback function** is a function passed as an argument to another function, which is then invoked after the completion of a task. This allows the program to continue executing while waiting for a time-consuming task to finish (such as reading a file or making an API request).

Example of a Callback Function:

```javascript

// Simulating a time-consuming task
function fetchData(callback) {
    setTimeout(() => {
        const data = "Fetched Data";
        callback(data);
    }, 2000);    // Waits 2 seconds before executing the callback
}

// Using the callback
fetchData(function(result) {
    console.log(result);    // Outputs: "Fetched Data" after 2 seconds
});
```

Key Points:

- Callbacks are commonly used in asynchronous operations like reading files, making network requests, or interacting with databases.
- However, the use of nested callbacks (sometimes referred to as "callback hell") can lead to complex and hard-to-maintain code, especially when multiple asynchronous tasks are involved.

Promises

A **promise** is a modern way of handling asynchronous operations. It represents a value that may be available now, or in the future, or never. A promise has three states:

- **Pending**: The initial state, neither fulfilled nor rejected.
- **Fulfilled**: The operation was successful, and the promise has a result.
- **Rejected**: The operation failed, and the promise has an error.

Creating and Using Promises:

```javascript
let fetchData = new Promise((resolve, reject) =>
{
    let success = true; // Simulating success or
failure of an operation

    setTimeout(() => {
        if (success) {
            resolve("Data               fetched
successfully!");
        } else {
            reject("Error fetching data.");
        }
    }, 2000);
```

```
});

// Handling the promise result
fetchData
    .then(result => {
        console.log(result);    // Outputs: "Data
fetched successfully!" after 2 seconds
    })
    .catch(error => {
        console.log(error);    // If there is an
error, it will be caught here
    });
```

Key Points:

- Promises provide a cleaner and more manageable way of handling asynchronous code than callbacks, especially when multiple asynchronous operations are chained together.
- The `.then()` method is called when the promise is fulfilled, and `.catch()` is called if the promise is rejected.
- Promises allow for better error handling and cleaner code compared to nested callbacks.

Async/Await

`async` and `await` are syntax enhancements introduced in ES2017 (ES8) that make working with promises even easier. An `async` function always returns a promise, and within that function, `await` is used to pause execution until the promise is resolved or rejected.

Using Async/Await:

```javascript
// An asynchronous function that uses await
async function fetchData() {
    let success = true; // Simulating success or failure of an operation
    try {
        const result = await new Promise((resolve, reject) => {
            setTimeout(() => {
                if (success) {
                    resolve("Data fetched successfully!");
                } else {
                    reject("Error fetching data.");
                }
            }, 2000);
        });
        console.log(result);   // Outputs: "Data fetched successfully!" after 2 seconds
    } catch (error) {
```

```
        console.log(error);    // If there's an
error, it will be caught here
    }
}


// Calling the async function
fetchData();
```

Key Points:

- `async` makes a function return a promise, and `await` pauses execution until the promise is resolved or rejected.
- `async/await` allows for asynchronous code to be written in a way that looks synchronous, making it easier to read and maintain.
- The `try...catch` block is used to handle errors when working with `async/await`.

How to Manage Asynchronous Operations Effectively

While `callbacks`, `promises`, and `async/await` are powerful tools, managing multiple asynchronous operations requires careful consideration. Here are some strategies for managing asynchronous operations effectively:

1. **Avoid Callback Hell**:

○ Callback hell can occur when you nest multiple callbacks within each other. To avoid this, consider using promises or `async/await`, as they help flatten your code structure.

2. **Promise.all() and Promise.race()**:

○ `Promise.all()` allows you to wait for multiple promises to resolve at once, which is especially useful when you need to execute several independent asynchronous tasks and wait for all of them to complete.

```javascript

let promise1 = fetchData();
let promise2 = fetchData();
Promise.all([promise1, promise2])
    .then(results => {
        console.log(results);     //
Outputs the results of both promises
    })
    .catch(error => {
        console.log(error);    // If
any promise is rejected, this will be
triggered
    });
```

○ `Promise.race()` allows you to wait for the first promise to settle (either fulfilled or rejected).

74

javascript

```
let promise1 = new Promise((resolve,
reject) => setTimeout(resolve, 100,
"First"));
let promise2 = new Promise((resolve,
reject) => setTimeout(resolve, 200,
"Second"));

Promise.race([promise1, promise2])
    .then(result => {
        console.log(result);        //
Outputs: "First" (since it resolves
first)
    });
```

3. **Error Handling**:

   o Proper error handling is essential when working with asynchronous operations. Always handle errors with `.catch()` for promises or `try...catch` for `async/await` to prevent unhandled promise rejections.

Real-World Example: Fetching Data from an API and Displaying It Dynamically

Let's now apply what we've learned about asynchronous programming by building a real-world example where we fetch data from an API and dynamically display it on a webpage. We'll use the **JSONPlaceholder** API, which provides free fake data for testing.

html

```
<!DOCTYPE html>
<html lang="en">
<head>
    <meta charset="UTF-8">
    <meta name="viewport" content="width=device-
width, initial-scale=1.0">
    <title>Fetch API Example</title>
</head>
<body>
    <h1>Posts from JSONPlaceholder</h1>
    <ul id="postsList"></ul>

    <script>
        // Function to fetch data from the API
        async function fetchPosts() {
            try {
                // Fetching data from the API
```

```
            const      response    =      await
fetch('https://jsonplaceholder.typicode.com/pos
ts');
            const      posts       =      await
response.json(); // Parsing the JSON response

            // Displaying the fetched posts
            const      postsList          =
document.getElementById('postsList');
            posts.forEach(post => {
            const      listItem          =
document.createElement('li');
            listItem.textContent          =
post.title;  // Displaying the title of each post

postsList.appendChild(listItem);
            });
        } catch (error) {
            console.error("Error     fetching
data: ", error);  // Handling any errors
            }
        }


        // Call the fetchPosts function when the
page loads
        fetchPosts();
    </script>
</body>
</html>
```

Explanation of the Code:

- **`fetchPosts` function**:
    - The `fetchPosts` function is asynchronous and uses `await` to wait for the response from the `fetch` API call.
    - After the data is fetched, it's parsed into JSON using `.json()`, and then we loop through the posts to display them in a list.
- **`try...catch`**:
    - This ensures that any errors (like network issues or invalid data) are caught and handled, preventing the app from crashing.
- **Dynamic Content**:
    - The content from the API (in this case, post titles) is dynamically added to the webpage inside an unordered list.

Conclusion

In this chapter, we covered:

- **Callback functions**: A way to handle asynchronous operations but with limitations like callback hell.

- **Promises**: A more manageable approach to handling asynchronous tasks, with improved error handling and chaining capabilities.

- **Async/Await**: The most modern and clean way to work with promises, making asynchronous code look synchronous, with easy-to-understand syntax.

- **Managing multiple asynchronous operations**: Techniques like `Promise.all()`, `Promise.race()`, and proper error handling help manage complex async flows.

Finally, we used these concepts to build a real-world application where we fetched data from an API and displayed it dynamically on a web page. In the next chapter, we will dive deeper into **JavaScript events** and **DOM manipulation** to enhance our web applications even further.

CHAPTER 7

ERROR HANDLING AND DEBUGGING

Error handling and debugging are essential skills for developers. Writing error-free code is virtually impossible, but how you handle errors can significantly improve the reliability of your application. In this chapter, we'll explore **try-catch blocks**, **error objects**, and **debugging techniques** to help you identify, handle, and fix errors effectively. We'll also implement error handling in a real-world application to demonstrate these concepts.

Try-Catch Blocks and Error Objects

Try-Catch Blocks

In JavaScript, **try-catch blocks** allow you to handle runtime errors in a controlled way. The **try** block contains the code that might throw an error, while the **catch** block contains the code to handle the error if one occurs. This approach prevents the program from crashing and lets you display meaningful messages or take corrective actions when an error happens.

Basic Structure:

```javascript

try {
    // Code that might throw an error
    let result = someFunction();
    console.log(result);
} catch (error) {
    // Code that runs if an error occurs
    console.error("Error        occurred:        ",
error.message);
}
```

Key Points:

- The code inside the `try` block is executed normally.
- If an error occurs, control is transferred to the `catch` block, where the error can be handled.
- **error.message** provides the error message, and **error.stack** gives the stack trace (which shows where the error occurred).

Error Objects

The `error` object contains information about the error that occurred. It can provide several properties, such as:

- **message**: A description of the error.
- **name**: The type of error (e.g., `TypeError`, `ReferenceError`).

81

- **stack**: A string representing the point in the code at which the error was created, useful for debugging.

Example of an Error Object:

javascript

```
try {
    let x = undefinedVariable;
} catch (error) {
    console.log(error.name);                    //
"ReferenceError"
    console.log(error.message);                 //
"undefinedVariable is not defined"
    console.log(error.stack);   // Stack trace
}
```

Debugging Techniques and Best Practices

Debugging is the process of finding and fixing bugs (or errors) in your code. Here are some best practices and techniques to help you debug your JavaScript applications effectively:

1. Using Console Statements

One of the simplest ways to debug is to use `console.log()`, `console.error()`, and `console.warn()` to inspect values, track the flow of execution, and identify errors.

Example:

```javascript
function calculateSum(a, b) {
    console.log("a:", a, "b:", b);   // Logs the
values of a and b
    return a + b;
}

console.log(calculateSum(5, 3));   // Outputs the
values and the result
```

- **`console.log()`**: For general information about variables, objects, and functions.
- **`console.error()`**: For logging error messages.
- **`console.warn()`**: For logging warnings about potential issues.

2. Breakpoints and the Browser's Developer Tools

Most modern browsers come with built-in **developer tools** that include a debugger. You can set breakpoints in your code, pause execution, inspect variables, and step through your code line by line.

- **Chrome DevTools**: Press F12 (or right-click and select "Inspect") to open the DevTools panel. Go to the **Sources** tab to set breakpoints.

- **Firefox Developer Tools**: Similar functionality is available in Firefox. Press F12 to open the Developer Tools.

3. Using the debugger Statement

The debugger statement can be placed directly in your code, and it will pause execution when the browser's debugger is open. This allows you to inspect the state of the application at that specific point.

```javascript
function add(a, b) {
    debugger;  // Execution will pause here when DevTools are open
    return a + b;
}
add(5, 3);
```

4. Inspecting Error Stacks

When an error occurs, using **error.stack** helps you track down where the error originated. Understanding the stack trace is essential for diagnosing issues, especially when working with asynchronous code.

Real-World Example: Implementing Error Handling in a Real-World App

Let's build a simple application that fetches data from an API, and we'll implement error handling to manage network errors, invalid data, and other potential issues.

Scenario: We're creating a to-do list app that fetches to-do items from the **JSONPlaceholder** API. We will handle potential errors such as network failure or invalid data format.

html

```html
<!DOCTYPE html>
<html lang="en">
<head>
    <meta charset="UTF-8">
    <meta name="viewport" content="width=device-width, initial-scale=1.0">
    <title>To-Do List</title>
</head>
<body>
    <h1>To-Do List</h1>
    <ul id="todoList"></ul>

    <script>
        // Function to fetch to-do items from the API
        async function fetchTodos() {
```

```
      try {
            const    response   =    await
fetch('https://jsonplaceholder.typicode.com/tod
os');

            // Check if the response is okay
(status code 200)
            if (!response.ok) {
                  throw  new  Error('Failed  to
fetch data. Status: ' + response.status);
            }

            // Parse the response data
            const    todos    =     await
response.json();

            // Check if the data is in the
expected format
            if (!Array.isArray(todos)) {
                  throw new Error('Data is not
in the expected format.');
            }

            // Display the to-do items in the
UI
            const        todoList        =
document.getElementById('todoList');
            todos.forEach(todo => {
```

```
                const        li        =
document.createElement('li');
                li.textContent = todo.title;
                todoList.appendChild(li);
            });
        } catch (error) {
            // Catch and handle errors
            console.error('Error    occurred:
', error.message);
            alert('Something    went    wrong.
Please try again later.');
        }
    }


    // Call the fetchTodos function when the
page loads
    fetchTodos();
    </script>
</body>
</html>
```

Explanation of the Code:

- **Error Handling in Fetch**:
  - We wrap the `fetch()` call in a `try-catch` block to handle potential errors, such as network failures or server errors.

- If the response status is not `ok` (i.e., not in the 200 range), we throw an error with a custom message indicating the failure.

- **Data Format Check**:
  - After parsing the response into JSON, we verify that the data is in the expected format (an array). If it's not, we throw an error.

- **Displaying Errors**:
  - If an error occurs during fetching or processing the data, we catch it in the `catch` block and display a friendly error message using `alert()` and log the error using `console.error()`.

- **UI Updates**:
  - If everything works as expected, we loop through the fetched to-do items and dynamically create `<li>` elements to display each item in the list.

Conclusion

In this chapter, we learned how to handle errors gracefully in JavaScript using:

- **Try-catch blocks** to catch and handle exceptions.
- **Error objects** to gain detailed information about the error, including the type, message, and stack trace.

- **Debugging techniques** like `console.log()`, using breakpoints, the `debugger` statement, and inspecting error stacks to identify and fix bugs.

We also implemented error handling in a real-world example where we fetched data from an API and displayed it in a web application. By following these practices, we can build more robust and resilient applications that handle errors gracefully and provide better user experiences.

In the next chapter, we will dive deeper into **working with JavaScript events** and **event handling** to make your web applications more interactive.

CHAPTER 8

OBJECT-ORIENTED JAVASCRIPT

Object-Oriented Programming (OOP) is a programming paradigm that organizes software design around data, or **objects**, rather than functions and logic. JavaScript is an object-oriented language, meaning that it supports concepts such as **objects, classes**, and **inheritance**. In this chapter, we will dive deep into **Objects, Classes, Constructors**, and **Prototypal Inheritance**, and we'll demonstrate how these concepts are used in building a real-world application—a **shopping cart**.

Objects, Classes, and Constructors

Objects

An **object** is a collection of properties, where each property is a key-value pair. In JavaScript, objects are used to group related data and functionality together. Each property can hold any type of data: string, number, array, or even other objects or functions.

Example of an Object:

```javascript
const person = {
```

```
    name: "Alice",
    age: 30,
    greet: function() {
        console.log("Hello, " + this.name);
    }
};


person.greet();   // Outputs: Hello, Alice
```

- **Properties**: name, age
- **Method**: greet() is a function that belongs to the person object.

Classes and Constructors

A **class** in JavaScript is a blueprint for creating objects. Classes can have properties (like an object) and methods (functions) that define the behavior of the objects created from the class. Classes were introduced in ES6, and they provide a more formal syntax for creating and working with objects.

A **constructor** is a special method for initializing new objects created from the class.

Example of a Class with a Constructor:

```
javascript


class Person {
```

```
constructor(name, age) {
    this.name = name;
    this.age = age;
}

greet() {
    console.log("Hello, " + this.name);
}
}

const person1 = new Person("Alice", 30);
const person2 = new Person("Bob", 25);

person1.greet();  // Outputs: Hello, Alice
person2.greet();  // Outputs: Hello, Bob
```

Key Points:

- The `constructor` method is automatically called when a new object is created using the `new` keyword.
- The `this` keyword inside the constructor refers to the new object being created.

Prototypal Inheritance and ES6 Classes

In JavaScript, **inheritance** allows one object to inherit properties and methods from another object. JavaScript uses **prototypal**

inheritance, which means that objects can directly inherit from other objects.

Prototypal Inheritance

Every JavaScript object has a prototype object, and it can access properties and methods defined on its prototype. This allows for shared behavior across multiple instances.

Example of Prototypal Inheritance:

```javascript
const animal = {
    speak() {
        console.log("Animal makes a sound");
    }
};

const dog = Object.create(animal);    // dog inherits from animal
dog.speak();   // Outputs: Animal makes a sound

dog.bark = function() {
    console.log("Woof!");
};

dog.bark();   // Outputs: Woof!
```

In the example above:

- The `dog` object inherits the `speak` method from the `animal` object.
- We add a new method, `bark`, to the `dog` object.

Inheritance in ES6 Classes

In ES6, you can use the `extends` keyword to create a class that inherits from another class. This simplifies the process of inheritance and makes the code more readable.

Example of Inheritance with ES6 Classes:

```javascript
javascript

class Animal {
    constructor(name) {
        this.name = name;
    }

    speak() {
        console.log(this.name + " makes a
sound");
    }
}

class Dog extends Animal {
    constructor(name, breed) {
```

```
        super(name);   // Call the parent class's
constructor
        this.breed = breed;
    }

    bark() {
        console.log(this.name + " barks!");
    }
}

const myDog = new Dog("Buddy", "Golden
Retriever");
myDog.speak();   // Outputs: Buddy makes a sound
myDog.bark();    // Outputs: Buddy barks!
```

Key Points:

- extends is used to create a subclass (a class that inherits from another).
- super() is used to call the constructor of the parent class.
- Methods from the parent class are inherited by the subclass.

Real-World Example: Building a Shopping Cart with Object-Oriented Principles

Let's apply the principles of object-oriented programming to build a simple **shopping cart** application. The shopping cart will allow users to add products, remove products, and view the total price of the items in the cart.

Example: Shopping Cart

javascript

```javascript
// Product class
class Product {
    constructor(name, price) {
        this.name = name;
        this.price = price;
    }
}

// ShoppingCart class
class ShoppingCart {
    constructor() {
        this.items = [];
    }

    // Add product to cart
    addProduct(product) {
        this.items.push(product);
        console.log(product.name + " added to the cart.");
    }

    // Remove product from cart
```

```javascript
    removeProduct(productName) {
        const index = this.items.findIndex(item
=> item.name === productName);
        if (index !== -1) {
            const        removedProduct        =
this.items.splice(index, 1);
            console.log(removedProduct[0].name +
" removed from the cart.");
        } else {
            console.log("Product   not   found   in
the cart.");
        }
    }


    // Get  total  price  of  all  products  in  the
cart
    getTotalPrice() {
        let total = 0;
        this.items.forEach(item => {
            total += item.price;
        });
        return total;
    }


    // Display all products in the cart
    displayCart() {
        if (this.items.length === 0) {
            console.log("Your cart is empty.");
        } else {
```

```
                console.log("Your cart contains:");
                this.items.forEach(item => {
                    console.log(item.name + ": $" +
item.price);
                });
            }
        }
    }

// Creating products
const laptop = new Product("Laptop", 1200);
const phone = new Product("Smartphone", 800);
const headphones = new Product("Headphones",
150);

// Creating shopping cart and adding products
const cart = new ShoppingCart();
cart.addProduct(laptop);
cart.addProduct(phone);
cart.addProduct(headphones);

// Display the cart and total price
cart.displayCart();
console.log("Total       price:       $"       +
cart.getTotalPrice());

// Remove a product and display the updated cart
cart.removeProduct("Smartphone");
cart.displayCart();
```

```
console.log("Updated    total    price:    $"    +
cart.getTotalPrice());
```

Explanation of the Shopping Cart Example:

1. **Product Class**:
   - The `Product` class defines the structure of a product, with properties like `name` and `price`.
2. **ShoppingCart Class**:
   - The `ShoppingCart` class manages a list of products (`this.items`) and provides methods for adding and removing products.
   - **addProduct()**: Adds a product to the cart.
   - **removeProduct()**: Removes a product by its name using `findIndex()` to locate the product and `splice()` to remove it.
   - **getTotalPrice()**: Calculates and returns the total price of all products in the cart.
   - **displayCart()**: Displays the current contents of the cart, including each product's name and price.
3. **Usage**:
   - We create several `Product` objects and add them to the `ShoppingCart` instance.
   - The cart displays its contents and total price. Then, we remove a product and update the cart display and total price.

Conclusion

In this chapter, we explored key Object-Oriented JavaScript concepts:

- **Objects**: Used to store related data and functionality.
- **Classes and Constructors**: Introduced a more structured way to create objects and initialize their properties.
- **Prototypal Inheritance**: How objects can inherit behavior from other objects.
- **ES6 Classes and Inheritance**: Modern syntax for working with classes and inheritance.
- **Real-World Example**: We applied these concepts to create a simple shopping cart that uses object-oriented principles to manage products and calculate total prices.

By understanding these principles, you can write more modular, scalable, and maintainable JavaScript code, which is essential for building complex applications. In the next chapter, we will explore more advanced JavaScript topics, such as **functional programming** and **design patterns**.

CHAPTER 9

JAVASCRIPT AND THE DOM

In this chapter, we will explore how JavaScript interacts with the **Document Object Model (DOM)**, a crucial concept for web development. The DOM represents the structure of an HTML document as a tree of objects, allowing JavaScript to manipulate elements on the page dynamically. We'll cover how to select, modify, and interact with DOM elements using JavaScript, and apply this knowledge in a real-world example of creating a **dynamic photo gallery**.

Introduction to the Document Object Model (DOM)

The **Document Object Model (DOM)** is a programming interface for web documents. It represents the structure of a web page as a tree of nodes, where each node corresponds to an element or a piece of content on the page. JavaScript can manipulate the DOM to update the content, structure, and styles of a webpage dynamically.

Key Points about the DOM:

- The DOM treats HTML and XML documents as a tree structure, where each element is a node.

- It allows JavaScript to read and update the content and structure of web pages in real-time.
- The DOM is **language-agnostic**, meaning it can be used with any programming language that can interface with it. In this case, we use JavaScript.

For example, consider the following simple HTML document:

```
html
```

```
<!DOCTYPE html>
<html lang="en">
<head>
    <meta charset="UTF-8">
    <meta name="viewport" content="width=device-width, initial-scale=1.0">
    <title>DOM Example</title>
</head>
<body>
    <h1>Hello, World!</h1>
    <p>This is a simple page.</p>
</body>
</html>
```

In the DOM, this structure is represented as a tree with nodes like `<html>`, `<body>`, `<h1>`, and `<p>`.

Manipulating the DOM with JavaScript

JavaScript provides several methods to interact with the DOM. We can **select**, **modify**, **delete**, and **add** elements dynamically. Here are some key operations:

Selecting DOM Elements

To manipulate elements on the page, we first need to select them. JavaScript provides various methods for selecting DOM elements:

1. **getElementById()**: Selects an element by its `id` attribute.

   ```javascript
   const header = document.getElementById("header");
   ```

2. **getElementsByClassName()**: Selects elements by their `class` name.

   ```javascript
   const paragraphs = document.getElementsByClassName("text");
   ```

3. **getElementsByTagName()**: Selects elements by their tag name.

103

```javascript
const              divs              =
document.getElementsByTagName("div");
```

4. **querySelector()**: Selects the first matching element using CSS selectors.

```javascript
const        firstParagraph        =
document.querySelector("p");
```

5. **querySelectorAll()**: Selects all matching elements using CSS selectors.

```javascript
const              allDivs              =
document.querySelectorAll("div");
```

Modifying DOM Elements

Once we have selected an element, we can modify it using JavaScript. Some common properties and methods include:

1. **Changing Text Content**:

```javascript
javascript
```

```
const            heading            =
document.querySelector("h1");
heading.textContent = "New Heading Text";
```

2. **Changing HTML Content**:

```javascript
const            paragraph            =
document.querySelector("p");
paragraph.innerHTML  =  "<strong>This  is
bold text</strong>";
```

3. **Changing Styles**:

```javascript
const div = document.querySelector("div");
div.style.backgroundColor = "lightblue";
div.style.fontSize = "20px";
```

4. **Adding and Removing Classes**:

```javascript
const            button            =
document.querySelector("button");
button.classList.add("active");
button.classList.remove("inactive");
```

Handling Events

JavaScript also allows us to handle events, such as clicks, form submissions, or key presses. Event listeners enable us to respond to user actions in real-time.

Example of Event Handling:

```javascript
const button = document.querySelector("button");

button.addEventListener("click", function() {
    alert("Button clicked!");
});
```

Common Event Types:

- `click`: Triggered when an element is clicked.
- `mouseover`: Triggered when the mouse pointer is over an element.
- `submit`: Triggered when a form is submitted.
- `keydown`, `keyup`: Triggered when a key is pressed or released.

Real-World Example: Creating a Dynamic Photo Gallery with JavaScript

Let's put the DOM manipulation skills we've learned into practice by creating a **dynamic photo gallery**. We'll allow users to add new images to the gallery by interacting with the page. The gallery will dynamically update when a user submits an image URL.

HTML Structure:

html

```
<!DOCTYPE html>
<html lang="en">
<head>
    <meta charset="UTF-8">
    <meta name="viewport" content="width=device-
width, initial-scale=1.0">
    <title>Photo Gallery</title>
    <style>
        #gallery {
            display: flex;
            flex-wrap: wrap;
        }
        .photo {
            margin: 10px;
            border: 2px solid #ccc;
            border-radius: 5px;
            width: 200px;
```

107

```
        height: 200px;
    }
    .photo img {
        width: 100%;
        height: 100%;
        border-radius: 5px;
    }
    </style>
</head>
<body>

<h1>Dynamic Photo Gallery</h1>
<input           type="text"          id="imageUrl"
placeholder="Enter Image URL" />
<button id="addImage">Add Image</button>
<div id="gallery"></div>

<script>
    // Select DOM elements
    const            imageUrlInput            =
document.getElementById("imageUrl");
    const            addButton            =
document.getElementById("addImage");
    const            gallery            =
document.getElementById("gallery");

    // Event listener for the 'Add Image' button
    addButton.addEventListener("click",
function() {
```

```
        const imageUrl = imageUrlInput.value;

    if (imageUrl) {
        // Create a new photo container
        const          photoDiv          =
document.createElement("div");
        photoDiv.classList.add("photo");

        // Create an img element and set its
source
        const          imgElement          =
document.createElement("img");
        imgElement.src = imageUrl;

        // Append the img element to the
photo container
        photoDiv.appendChild(imgElement);

        // Append the photo container to the
gallery
        gallery.appendChild(photoDiv);

        // Clear the input field
        imageUrlInput.value = "";
    } else {
        alert("Please enter a valid image
URL!");
    }
});
```

```
</script>

</body>
</html>
```

Explanation of the Code:

1. **HTML**:
   o We have an `input` field for users to enter an image URL, a `button` to add the image, and a `div` with the `id="gallery"` where the images will be displayed.

2. **JavaScript**:
   o **Event Listener**: We add an event listener to the "Add Image" button. When the button is clicked, the `click` event triggers a function that reads the URL entered in the `input` field.
   o **DOM Manipulation**:
      ▪ If the URL is valid, a new `div` (with the class `photo`) is created for each image.
      ▪ An `img` element is created and its `src` attribute is set to the entered URL.
      ▪ The `img` element is added to the new `div`, which is then appended to the gallery.

110

      o **Dynamic Updates**: When the user adds an image, the gallery is updated in real-time without needing to refresh the page.

3. **CSS**:

      o The gallery items are displayed in a flexible grid layout using `flexbox`, and each image is displayed in a square format with rounded corners.

Conclusion

In this chapter, we covered:

- **The Document Object Model (DOM)**: Understanding the DOM as a tree of objects representing the structure of an HTML document.
- **DOM Manipulation**: How to select, modify, and interact with DOM elements using JavaScript, including text, styles, and event handling.
- **Real-World Example**: We created a dynamic photo gallery that allows users to add images by entering their URLs. This demonstrated how JavaScript can interact with HTML to update the page content dynamically.

By mastering these concepts, you can build interactive and dynamic web applications. In the next chapter, we will dive into **advanced topics in JavaScript** such as **asynchronous programming** and **promises** to handle tasks like fetching data from APIs.

CHAPTER 10

EVENT HANDLING AND DOM MANIPULATION

In this chapter, we'll explore **event handling** and **DOM manipulation** in more detail. Events are a key part of creating interactive web applications. By understanding how to listen for events like clicks, form submissions, and keypresses, you can build dynamic web pages. We'll also cover **event delegation** and **event bubbling**, which help improve performance and flexibility when dealing with multiple elements. We'll apply these concepts by building a real-world example: **an interactive form with live validation**.

Understanding Events: Click, Submit, Keypress

An **event** is any interaction that happens within the browser, such as a user clicking a button, typing in a form, or submitting a form. In JavaScript, we can "listen" for these events and define functions that should be executed when the event occurs.

Click Event

The `click` event is triggered when an element (such as a button or a link) is clicked by the user.

Example:

```javascript
const button = document.getElementById("submitButton");

button.addEventListener("click", function() {
    console.log("Button was clicked!");
});
```

Submit Event

The `submit` event occurs when a form is submitted, either by clicking the submit button or pressing Enter inside a form field.

Example:

```javascript
const form = document.getElementById("myForm");

form.addEventListener("submit", function(event) {
{
```

```
    event.preventDefault(); // Prevents the form
from submitting and refreshing the page
    console.log("Form submitted!");
});
```

Keypress Event

The `keypress` event is triggered when a user presses a key on the keyboard while an element (such as an input field) is focused.

Example:

javascript

```
const             inputField            =
document.getElementById("username");

inputField.addEventListener("keypress",
function(event) {
    console.log("Key pressed: " + event.key);
});
```

Event Delegation and Bubbling

Event Bubbling

Event **bubbling** is a mechanism where an event starts at the most specific node (the target) and then bubbles up to the root. For example, if you click on an element inside a container, the event will first trigger on the clicked element and then propagate upwards through its parent elements.

Example:

html

```
<div id="parent">
    <button id="child">Click me!</button>
</div>

<script>

document.getElementById("parent").addEventListener("click", function(event) {
        console.log("Parent clicked!");
    });


document.getElementById("child").addEventListener("click", function(event) {
        console.log("Child clicked!");
    });
</script>
```

Output:

nginx

Child clicked!

116

```
Parent clicked!
```

In the above example, when the button is clicked, both the `child` and `parent` event listeners are triggered due to event bubbling.

Event Delegation

Event **delegation** is a technique where you attach a single event listener to a parent element instead of attaching one to each child element. This is useful when dealing with dynamic content (e.g., adding/removing elements) or a large number of elements.

Instead of attaching event listeners to multiple individual child elements, you attach a single listener to the parent and rely on event bubbling to catch events on the children.

Example:

```html
html

<ul id="todoList">
    <li>Task 1</li>
    <li>Task 2</li>
    <li>Task 3</li>
</ul>

<script>
```

```
document.getElementById("todoList").addEventLis
tener("click", function(event) {
        if (event.target.tagName === "LI") {
            console.log("You   clicked   on:   "   +
event.target.textContent);
        }
    });
</script>
```

Explanation:

- Instead of adding a click listener to each <li>, we add one to the parent <ul>.
- When a user clicks on a list item, the event bubbles up to the ul element, where the listener is attached. The event handler then checks if the clicked target is an <li>.

Advantages of Event Delegation:

- More efficient for handling events on a large number of child elements.
- Dynamically added elements don't need separate event listeners.

Real-World Example: Building an Interactive Form with Live Validation

In this example, we will build a form with live validation. As the user types into the input fields, we will dynamically validate the input and display appropriate feedback.

HTML Structure:

html

```
<!DOCTYPE html>
<html lang="en">
<head>
    <meta charset="UTF-8">
    <meta name="viewport" content="width=device-
width, initial-scale=1.0">
    <title>Interactive Form</title>
    <style>
        .valid { border-color: green; }
        .invalid { border-color: red; }
        .error-message { color: red; font-size:
0.9em; }
    </style>
</head>
<body>

<h1>Interactive Form</h1>
<form id="myForm">
```

```
    <label for="email">Email:</label>
    <input type="email" id="email" name="email"
required>
    <span      id="emailError"      class="error-
message"></span><br><br>

    <label for="password">Password:</label>
    <input      type="password"      id="password"
name="password" required>
    <span      id="passwordError"      class="error-
message"></span><br><br>

    <button type="submit">Submit</button>
</form>

<script>
    // Select the form and input elements
    const              form              =
document.getElementById("myForm");
    const              emailInput              =
document.getElementById("email");
    const              passwordInput              =
document.getElementById("password");
    const              emailError              =
document.getElementById("emailError");
    const              passwordError              =
document.getElementById("passwordError");

    // Event listener for live validation
```

```
    emailInput.addEventListener("input",
function() {
        const emailValue = emailInput.value;
        if (!emailValue.match(/^[^ ]+@[^ ]+\.[a-
z]{2,3}$/)) {

emailInput.classList.add("invalid");

emailInput.classList.remove("valid");
            emailError.textContent  =  "Please
enter a valid email address.";
        } else {

emailInput.classList.remove("invalid");
            emailInput.classList.add("valid");
            emailError.textContent = "";
        }
    });

    passwordInput.addEventListener("input",
function() {
        const          passwordValue          =
passwordInput.value;
        if (passwordValue.length < 6) {

passwordInput.classList.add("invalid");

passwordInput.classList.remove("valid");
```

```
            passwordError.textContent        =
"Password must be at least 6 characters long.";
        } else {

passwordInput.classList.remove("invalid");

passwordInput.classList.add("valid");
            passwordError.textContent = "";
        }
    });

    // Form submit event
    form.addEventListener("submit",
function(event) {
        // Prevent form submission if there are
validation errors
        if
(emailInput.classList.contains("invalid")      ||
passwordInput.classList.contains("invalid")) {
            event.preventDefault();
            alert("Please fix the errors before
submitting the form.");
        } else {
            alert("Form              submitted
successfully!");
        }
    });
</script>
```

```
</body>
</html>
```

Explanation of the Code:

1. **HTML**:
   - We have a simple form with two fields: **Email** and **Password**.
   - Each input field has an associated `span` element for displaying error messages.
   - The form contains a submit button, which will trigger validation when clicked.

2. **JavaScript**:
   - We attach **input** event listeners to the email and password fields. The `input` event is fired every time the user types something in the input field.
   - **Email Validation**: When the user types in the email field, we check if the input matches a regular expression pattern for a valid email address. If invalid, we show an error message and apply a red border.
   - **Password Validation**: We check if the password is at least 6 characters long. If it's too short, we show an error message and apply a red border.
   - **Form Submission**: Before the form is submitted, we check if any of the fields have the `invalid`

class. If there are errors, we prevent the form submission and show an alert.

3. **CSS**:

   o   We use classes `.valid` and `.invalid` to change the border color of the input fields based on their validity.

   o   Error messages are styled with the `.error-message` class in red font.

Conclusion

In this chapter, we:

- **Learned about event handling** in JavaScript, including `click`, `submit`, and `keypress` events.

- **Explored event delegation** and **event bubbling**, understanding how events propagate through the DOM and how we can use delegation to optimize event handling for dynamic content.

- **Built a real-world interactive form** with live validation that provides real-time feedback to the user.

By mastering event handling and DOM manipulation, you can create rich, interactive user interfaces that respond to user actions in real-time. In the next chapter, we will explore **advanced**

JavaScript concepts like **asynchronous programming** and **fetching data from APIs** to build even more powerful applications.

CHAPTER 11

BUILDING YOUR FIRST INTERACTIVE WEB APP

In this chapter, we will dive into the fundamentals of building your first interactive web app. Specifically, we will learn how to structure a **single-page application (SPA)**, combine **HTML, CSS**, and **JavaScript** to create interactive web pages, and build a **real-world example**: a **basic weather app** using **JavaScript** and an **API**.

Structuring a Simple Single-Page App (SPA)

A **Single-Page Application (SPA)** is a web app that loads a single HTML page and dynamically updates the content based on user interaction. Unlike traditional multi-page applications, SPAs do not require full page reloads. Instead, they fetch data from the server asynchronously and update parts of the page without refreshing the whole page.

Core Elements of a SPA:

- **HTML**: Provides the structure and layout of the page.
- **CSS**: Styles the page and provides the visual design.

- **JavaScript**: Handles dynamic behavior and interaction, such as fetching data from APIs and updating the DOM.

Basic SPA Structure:

An SPA typically includes the following components:

- **index.html**: The main HTML file where the app is rendered.
- **styles.css**: A CSS file that contains the styles for the app.
- **script.js**: A JavaScript file that manages dynamic content and functionality.

Using HTML, CSS, and JavaScript Together for Interactive Web Pages

To build an interactive web page, HTML, CSS, and JavaScript need to work together:

- **HTML** defines the structure of the page, including headers, input fields, buttons, and other elements.
- **CSS** is used to style these elements, making the app visually appealing and responsive.
- **JavaScript** adds interactivity, such as handling user inputs, fetching data, and dynamically updating the DOM without reloading the page.

Example of a Basic Web Page Structure:

html

```html
<!DOCTYPE html>
<html lang="en">
<head>
    <meta charset="UTF-8">
    <meta name="viewport" content="width=device-width, initial-scale=1.0">
    <title>Weather App</title>
    <link rel="stylesheet" href="styles.css">
</head>
<body>
    <div id="app">
        <h1>Weather App</h1>
        <input type="text" id="cityInput" placeholder="Enter city">
        <button id="getWeatherButton">Get Weather</button>
        <div id="weatherInfo"></div>
    </div>
    <script src="script.js"></script>
</body>
</html>
```

- **HTML**: The structure includes an input field for entering the city name, a button to fetch the weather, and a div to display the weather information.

- **CSS**: We will apply styles to make the app look neat and responsive.
- **JavaScript**: The script will handle the fetching of weather data and updating the UI dynamically based on the API response.

Real-World Example: A Basic Weather App Using JavaScript and an API

Now that we've covered the basic structure of a SPA, let's build a simple **weather app** using **JavaScript** and the **OpenWeatherMap API**. This app will allow users to enter a city, click a button to fetch weather data, and display the results dynamically on the page.

Step 1: Get API Key from OpenWeatherMap

1. Go to OpenWeatherMap.
2. Sign up for a free account and obtain an API key to access the weather data.

Step 2: HTML Structure (already covered)

We already have the basic structure for the weather app in the `index.html` file from earlier. Now, we need to implement the functionality in **JavaScript**.

Step 3: JavaScript Functionality

In this example, we will:

1. Fetch weather data from the OpenWeatherMap API using the `fetch()` method.
2. Update the DOM to display the weather information dynamically.

```javascript
// script.js

const getWeatherButton =
document.getElementById("getWeatherButton");
const cityInput =
document.getElementById("cityInput");
const weatherInfo =
document.getElementById("weatherInfo");

const apiKey = "YOUR_API_KEY";  // Replace with
your OpenWeatherMap API key

// Function to fetch weather data
async function getWeather(city) {
    try {
        const response = await
fetch(`https://api.openweathermap.org/data/2.5/
```

```
weather?q=${city}&appid=${apiKey}&units=metric`
);

        if (!response.ok) {
            throw new Error("City not found");
        }

        const data = await response.json();
        displayWeather(data);
    } catch (error) {
        weatherInfo.textContent = "Error: " +
error.message;
    }
}

// Function to display weather data
function displayWeather(data) {
    const { name, main, weather } = data;
    const temperature = main.temp;
    const description = weather[0].description;

    weatherInfo.innerHTML = `
        <h2>${name}</h2>
        <p>Temperature: ${temperature}°C</p>
        <p>Condition: ${description}</p>
    `;
}

// Event listener for button click
```

```
getWeatherButton.addEventListener("click",
function() {
    const city = cityInput.value.trim();
    if (city) {
        getWeather(city);
    } else {
        weatherInfo.textContent = "Please enter
a city name.";
    }
});
```

Explanation:

- **getWeather()**: This function fetches weather data from the OpenWeatherMap API. It uses the fetch() method to send a request to the API with the city name and API key. The response is parsed as JSON and passed to the displayWeather() function.

- **displayWeather()**: This function dynamically updates the DOM with the weather data. It extracts the temperature and weather condition from the response and displays them.

- **Error Handling**: If the city is not found or if there's any issue with the API request, an error message is displayed.

- **Event Listener**: We add an event listener to the "Get Weather" button. When clicked, it triggers the getWeather() function and passes the city name entered by the user.

Step 4: CSS Styling

To make the weather app look nice, let's add some basic styles.

css

```css
/* styles.css */

body {
    font-family: Arial, sans-serif;
    background-color: #f0f0f0;
    display: flex;
    justify-content: center;
    align-items: center;
    height: 100vh;
    margin: 0;
}

#app {
    background-color: #fff;
    padding: 20px;
    border-radius: 8px;
    box-shadow: 0 4px 6px rgba(0, 0, 0, 0.1);
    text-align: center;
    width: 300px;
}

input[type="text"] {
    padding: 10px;
    width: 100%;
```

133

```
        margin-bottom: 10px;
        border: 1px solid #ccc;
        border-radius: 4px;
}

button {
        padding: 10px 20px;
        background-color: #007bff;
        color: white;
        border: none;
        border-radius: 4px;
        cursor: pointer;
}

button:hover {
        background-color: #0056b3;
}

#error {
        color: red;
}

h1 {
        margin-bottom: 20px;
}
```

Explanation of the CSS:

- We center the `#app` container both horizontally and vertically using `flexbox`.
- The `input` field and `button` are styled to make the app look clean and user-friendly.
- When the button is hovered, the background color changes to indicate interactivity.

Conclusion

In this chapter, we:

- **Learned how to structure a simple Single-Page Application (SPA)** by combining HTML, CSS, and JavaScript.
- **Explored how to use JavaScript to fetch data from an API** and dynamically update the DOM.
- **Built a basic weather app** that allows users to input a city name, fetch weather data from the OpenWeatherMap API, and display the results on the page.

With this knowledge, you can start building more interactive and dynamic web applications. In the next chapter, we will explore **advanced topics** such as **state management**, **routing**, and **working with more complex APIs** to take your web development skills to the next level.

CHAPTER 12

USING APIS IN JAVASCRIPT

In modern web development, APIs (Application Programming Interfaces) are essential for building dynamic and interactive applications. APIs allow your app to communicate with other services and retrieve or send data. In this chapter, we'll explore how to interact with external APIs, fetch data, and display JSON results in your web application. We'll also implement a real-world example by integrating a **news API** into a simple app.

What is an API? How to Interact with External APIs

An **API** (Application Programming Interface) is a set of rules and protocols that allows different software applications to communicate with each other. In the context of web development, an API is often used to interact with remote servers or external services to retrieve or send data.

APIs are typically **RESTful** and use **HTTP** methods such as GET, POST, PUT, and DELETE to communicate. For example:

- **GET**: Retrieve data from the server.
- **POST**: Send data to the server.

- **PUT**: Update data on the server.
- **DELETE**: Remove data from the server.

Most APIs return data in the form of **JSON** (JavaScript Object Notation), which is a lightweight, easy-to-parse data format.

Common Example:

- Fetching weather data from a weather service API.
- Retrieving news articles from a news service API.
- Interacting with social media platforms like Twitter or Facebook through their respective APIs.

Fetching and Displaying JSON Data

To interact with APIs in JavaScript, we typically use the `fetch()` function. This function allows us to make HTTP requests and get the response data, often in **JSON** format.

Using `fetch()` to Retrieve Data from an API

The `fetch()` function returns a **Promise**, so we can use `.then()` or **async/await** to handle the response. Once the response is received, we can parse it as JSON and use it in our app.

Here's a simple example of how to use `fetch()` to retrieve data from an API:

137

```javascript
fetch('https://api.example.com/data')
    .then(response => response.json())  // Parse
the response as JSON
    .then(data => {
        console.log(data);  // Handle the data
    })
    .catch(error => {
        console.log("Error:", error);  // Handle
errors
    });
```

Handling Errors

When interacting with APIs, it's important to handle errors, such as when the API is down or when the request fails. Using `try...catch` or `.catch()` with Promises helps us manage these situations.

```javascript
fetch('https://api.example.com/data')
    .then(response => {
        if (!response.ok) {  // Check if the
response is successful
            throw new Error('Network response
was not ok');
        }
```

```
        return  response.json();   // Parse  the
response as JSON
    })
    .then(data => {
        console.log(data);  // Handle the data
    })
    .catch(error => {
        console.log("There was a problem with the
fetch operation:", error);   // Handle errors
    });
```

Using `async/await` for Cleaner Syntax

Instead of using `.then()`, you can use **async/await** for more readable and synchronous-like code:

javascript

```
async function getData() {
    try {
        const      response      =      await
fetch('https://api.example.com/data');
        if (!response.ok) {
            throw  new  Error('Network  response
was not ok');
        }
        const data = await response.json();   //
Parse the response as JSON
        console.log(data);  // Handle the data
    } catch (error) {
```

```
        console.log("Error:", error);  // Handle
errors
    }
}


getData();
```

Real-World Example: Integrating a News API into Your App

Let's build a **real-world application** where we fetch news articles from an API and display them dynamically on a webpage. We'll use the **NewsAPI**, which provides access to real-time news articles from various sources.

Step 1: Get API Key from NewsAPI

1. Visit NewsAPI.
2. Sign up for a free account and get your API key.

Step 2: HTML Structure

We will create a basic structure for our app where the user can click a button to load news articles, and the results will be displayed dynamically.

html

```
<!DOCTYPE html>
```

```html
<html lang="en">
<head>
    <meta charset="UTF-8">
    <meta name="viewport" content="width=device-
width, initial-scale=1.0">
    <title>News App</title>
    <style>
        body {
            font-family: Arial, sans-serif;
            margin: 0;
            padding: 20px;
            background-color: #f9f9f9;
        }
        h1 {
            text-align: center;
        }
        #articles {
            display: grid;
            grid-template-columns:      repeat(3,
1fr);
            gap: 20px;
            margin-top: 20px;
        }
        .article {
            background: white;
            padding: 15px;
            border-radius: 8px;
            box-shadow: 0 4px 6px rgba(0, 0, 0,
0.1);
```

```
        }
        .article img {
            width: 100%;
            border-radius: 5px;
        }
        .article h2 {
            font-size: 18px;
            color: #333;
        }
        .article p {
            font-size: 14px;
            color: #777;
        }
        button {
            display: block;
            width: 100%;
            padding: 10px;
            background-color: #007bff;
            color: white;
            font-size: 16px;
            border: none;
            border-radius: 5px;
            cursor: pointer;
        }
        button:hover {
            background-color: #0056b3;
        }
    </style>
</head>
```

```
<body>

    <h1>Latest News</h1>
    <button id="loadNews">Load News</button>

    <div id="articles"></div>

    <script src="script.js"></script>
</body>
</html>
```

Step 3: JavaScript Functionality

Now, let's use JavaScript to fetch news articles from the API and display them on the page.

```
javascript

// script.js

const apiKey = 'YOUR_API_KEY';  // Replace with
your NewsAPI key
const           loadNewsButton           =
document.getElementById('loadNews');
const            articlesDiv              =
document.getElementById('articles');

// Function to fetch and display news
async function getNews() {
    try {
```

143

```
        const       response      =        await
fetch(`https://newsapi.org/v2/top-
headlines?country=us&apiKey=${apiKey}`);
        if (!response.ok) {
            throw  new  Error('Failed  to  fetch
news');
        }
        const data = await response.json();
        displayNews(data.articles);
    } catch (error) {
        console.error('Error  fetching  news:',
error);
        articlesDiv.innerHTML      =      `<p>Error
fetching news. Please try again later.</p>`;
    }
}


// Function to display the fetched news articles
function displayNews(articles) {
    articlesDiv.innerHTML  =  '';     //  Clear
previous articles
    articles.forEach(article => {
        const          articleDiv           =
document.createElement('div');
        articleDiv.classList.add('article');
        articleDiv.innerHTML = `
            <img    src="${article.urlToImage}"
alt="News Image">
            <h2>${article.title}</h2>
```

```
        <p>${article.description}</p>
        <a            href="${article.url}"
target="_blank">Read more</a>
        `;
        articlesDiv.appendChild(articleDiv);
}


// Event listener for the "Load News" button
loadNewsButton.addEventListener('click',
getNews);
```

Explanation of the Code:

1. **HTML**:
   - We create a `button` element that, when clicked, will load the news.
   - The `div` with the `id="articles"` is where we will dynamically insert the news articles.

2. **JavaScript**:
   - `getNews()`: This asynchronous function uses the `fetch()` method to get data from the NewsAPI. It checks if the response is successful and then parses the JSON data.
   - `displayNews()`: This function dynamically generates the HTML for each news article and appends it to the page.

- o **Error Handling**: If there's an error while fetching the data, a message is displayed to the user.

3. **Styling**:
   - o We use **CSS Grid** to display the articles in a responsive grid layout.
   - o Each article is styled with a simple box, and images are displayed at the top of each article.

Conclusion

In this chapter, we:

- **Explored how to interact with APIs** using JavaScript, focusing on fetching data from a public API (NewsAPI).
- **Learned how to use `fetch()`** to retrieve and display data dynamically in our web application.
- **Built a real-world example of a news app** that fetches and displays the latest news articles.

With this knowledge, you can now integrate APIs into your own web applications, enabling you to create dynamic, data-driven websites. In the next chapter, we will explore **working with more advanced APIs** and using **authentication** to interact with protected resources.

CHAPTER 13

STATE MANAGEMENT AND WEB STORAGE

In this chapter, we will explore **state management** in web applications, and how to use **Web Storage** (including **localStorage**, **sessionStorage**, and **cookies**) to manage data persistently on the client-side. We'll also walk through a **real-world example** of saving **user preferences** in a web app, allowing for a personalized user experience.

Understanding State Management in a Web App

State management refers to how data is handled in an application and how changes to that data are reflected in the app's user interface (UI). In a **web app**, state can include:

- **User data**: Information such as login status, preferences, or settings.
- **UI state**: Information related to the app's layout, such as form inputs, button states, or modal visibility.
- **App data**: Data fetched from external APIs, like news articles, weather data, or social media posts.

147

Managing this state effectively is crucial for building interactive and user-friendly applications. However, web apps often require state to be preserved even when the user navigates between pages or refreshes the browser. This is where **client-side storage** solutions like **localStorage**, **sessionStorage**, and **cookies** come into play.

Using localStorage, sessionStorage, and Cookies

1. localStorage

`localStorage` is a web storage solution that allows you to store key-value pairs in the browser. The data stored in `localStorage` persists even after the user closes and reopens the browser, meaning it has **persistent** storage.

- **Storage Capacity**: Typically 5-10MB.
- **Lifetime**: Data persists until explicitly removed (manual removal or clearing browser data).

Example:

```javascript

// Storing data in localStorage
localStorage.setItem('theme', 'dark');

// Retrieving data from localStorage
```

```
const theme = localStorage.getItem('theme');
console.log(theme);   // Outputs: "dark"

// Removing data from localStorage
localStorage.removeItem('theme');

// Clearing all data in localStorage
localStorage.clear();
```

2. sessionStorage

sessionStorage is similar to localStorage, but it stores data only for the duration of the page session. This means that the data is cleared when the page or browser tab is closed, making it **temporary** storage.

- **Storage Capacity**: Typically 5-10MB.
- **Lifetime**: Data is cleared when the session ends (i.e., when the tab or browser is closed).

Example:

```
javascript
```

```
// Storing data in sessionStorage
sessionStorage.setItem('username', 'johnDoe');

// Retrieving data from sessionStorage
const                    username                    =
sessionStorage.getItem('username');
```

```
console.log(username);  // Outputs: "johnDoe"

// Removing data from sessionStorage
sessionStorage.removeItem('username');

// Clearing all data in sessionStorage
sessionStorage.clear();
```

3. Cookies

Cookies are small pieces of data that are stored in the user's browser and are sent to the server with every HTTP request. Cookies can store small amounts of data (around 4KB per cookie), and they can have an **expiration date**, allowing for data persistence beyond the session.

- **Storage Capacity**: Typically 4KB per cookie.
- **Lifetime**: Cookies can be set to expire at a specific time, allowing for temporary or long-term storage.

Example:

```javascript
// Setting a cookie with an expiration date
document.cookie = "user=JaneDoe; expires=Thu, 18 Dec 2025 12:00:00 UTC; path=/";

// Retrieving cookies (all cookies)
```

```
console.log(document.cookie);        //    Outputs:
"user=JaneDoe"

// Deleting a cookie by setting its expiration
date to a past date
document.cookie = "user=; expires=Thu, 01 Jan
1970 00:00:00 UTC; path=/";
```

- Cookies are mainly used for tracking, authentication, and session management. They can be sent with every HTTP request, which is why they're commonly used for things like **user sessions** or **tracking user behavior**.

Real-World Example: Saving User Preferences in a Web App

Let's build a simple example of a web app where users can choose a **theme preference** (light or dark). The app will save the user's preference using `localStorage`, and whenever the user returns to the page, the preference will be loaded, ensuring a consistent experience.

Step 1: HTML Structure

We'll create a basic page with a button to toggle the theme between light and dark.

```
html
```

```
<!DOCTYPE html>
<html lang="en">
<head>
    <meta charset="UTF-8">
    <meta name="viewport" content="width=device-
width, initial-scale=1.0">
    <title>User Preferences: Theme</title>
    <style>
        body {
            font-family: Arial, sans-serif;
            margin: 0;
            padding: 20px;
            transition:  background-color  0.3s,
color 0.3s;
        }
        .light {
            background-color: #fff;
            color: #000;
        }
        .dark {
            background-color: #333;
            color: #fff;
        }
        button {
            padding: 10px 20px;
            border: none;
            background-color: #007bff;
            color: white;
            cursor: pointer;
```

```
        font-size: 16px;
        border-radius: 5px;
    }
    button:hover {
        background-color: #0056b3;
    }
    </style>
</head>
<body>

<h1>Choose Your Theme</h1>
<button   id="toggleThemeButton">Switch   to   Dark
Mode</button>

<script src="script.js"></script>
</body>
</html>
```

Step 2: JavaScript Functionality

Now, let's write the JavaScript to toggle between light and dark themes and save the user's choice in `localStorage`.

```javascript
// script.js

// Get the elements
const              toggleButton              =
document.getElementById("toggleThemeButton");
```

```javascript
// Function to apply the theme
function applyTheme(theme) {
    document.body.classList.remove("light",
"dark");
    document.body.classList.add(theme);

    // Save the user's theme preference in
localStorage
    localStorage.setItem("theme", theme);

    // Update button text based on the current
theme
    toggleButton.textContent = theme === "dark"
? "Switch to Light Mode" : "Switch to Dark Mode";
}

// Check if a theme preference exists in
localStorage and apply it
const                   savedTheme                =
localStorage.getItem("theme");
if (savedTheme) {
    applyTheme(savedTheme);  // Apply saved theme
(light or dark)
} else {
    // Default to light theme if no preference is
saved
    applyTheme("light");
}
```

```
// Toggle theme when button is clicked
toggleButton.addEventListener("click",
function() {
    const           currentTheme        =
document.body.classList.contains("dark")         ?
"dark" : "light";
    const newTheme = currentTheme === "dark" ?
"light" : "dark";
    applyTheme(newTheme);
});
```

Explanation:

1. **HTML**:
   o We have a button labeled "Switch to Dark Mode", which will allow users to toggle between light and dark themes.

2. **JavaScript**:
   o **applyTheme()**: This function applies the specified theme (light or dark) to the body of the page by adding the corresponding class (light or dark).
   o **Saving Preferences**: When the theme is toggled, the chosen theme is saved in localStorage so that it persists across page reloads.
   o **Loading Preferences**: On page load, the script checks if there is a saved theme in

155

`localStorage` and applies it. If no preference is found, the default theme is light.

- o **Button Text Update**: The button's text updates dynamically to reflect the current theme.

Conclusion

In this chapter, we covered:

- **State Management**: How to manage state in a web app, including user preferences, UI state, and app data.
- **Web Storage**: We explored how to use `localStorage`, `sessionStorage`, and **cookies** to store data on the client side.
- **Real-World Example**: We built a simple app that saves the user's theme preference using `localStorage` and dynamically changes the theme between light and dark modes.

By using web storage, you can create more personalized and persistent user experiences in your web applications. In the next chapter, we will explore **advanced topics in front-end frameworks**, such as React or Vue.js, to take your web development skills further.

CHAPTER 14

WORKING WITH FORMS AND VALIDATION

Forms are a core part of many web applications, allowing users to input data such as personal details, feedback, or login credentials. Handling forms effectively and performing input validation are key aspects of ensuring that data is correctly submitted and processed. In this chapter, we will discuss how to **handle form submissions**, **validate form inputs dynamically**, and build a **real-world dynamic registration form** with validation.

Handling Form Submissions with JavaScript

When a user submits a form, you typically want to capture that data and process it—either by sending it to a server or performing actions in the browser. You can handle form submissions in JavaScript using **event listeners**.

Form Submission Using JavaScript

The `submit` event is triggered when a form is submitted. You can capture this event and prevent the default form submission using event.preventDefault(), allowing you to perform additional actions (like validation) before submitting the form.

Basic Example:

html

```html
<form id="registrationForm">
    <input        type="text"        id="username"
name="username" placeholder="Username">
    <input type="email" id="email" name="email"
placeholder="Email">
    <input        type="password"        id="password"
name="password" placeholder="Password">
    <button type="submit">Submit</button>
</form>

<script>
    const              form              =
document.getElementById("registrationForm");

    form.addEventListener("submit",
function(event) {
        event.preventDefault(); // Prevents form
from submitting immediately

        // Process form data or perform
validation
        console.log("Form submitted!");
```

```
    });
</script>
```

In this example:

- The form will **not** submit until the `submit` event handler runs.
- The `event.preventDefault()` method stops the default form submission, allowing you to process the data or validate it before sending it.

Validating Form Input Dynamically

Validating form inputs dynamically helps improve user experience by providing immediate feedback on incorrect inputs (e.g., missing required fields, invalid email format, password strength). You can achieve this using JavaScript.

1. Basic Input Validation

For simple validation, you can check whether required fields are filled, or if the input matches certain criteria (like a valid email or password).

Example of Validating Form Fields:

```
javascript
```

```javascript
const            usernameInput              =
document.getElementById("username");
const            emailInput                 =
document.getElementById("email");
const            passwordInput              =
document.getElementById("password");

form.addEventListener("submit",  function(event)
{
    event.preventDefault();

    let isValid = true;

    // Validate Username
    if (usernameInput.value.trim() === "") {
        isValid = false;
        alert("Username is required");
    }

    // Validate Email
    const emailRegex = /^[a-zA-Z0-9._-]+@[a-zA-
Z0-9.-]+\.[a-zA-Z]{2,6}$/;
    if (!emailRegex.test(emailInput.value)) {
        isValid = false;
        alert("Please    enter    a    valid    email
address");
    }

    // Validate Password
```

```
    if (passwordInput.value.length < 6) {
        isValid = false;
        alert("Password   must   be   at   least   6
characters long");
    }

    if (isValid) {
        // Submit the form or process data
        console.log("Form          is          valid.
Processing...");
    }
});
```

In this example:

- **Username** is required.
- **Email** must match a regular expression pattern for a valid email format.
- **Password** must be at least 6 characters long.

2. Real-time Validation (Dynamic Input Validation)

You can also validate inputs **as the user types**, providing immediate feedback (e.g., showing an error message below the field if the input is invalid).

Example of Real-time Validation:

```
javascript
```

```
const            usernameInput            =
document.getElementById("username");
const            usernameError            =
document.getElementById("usernameError");

usernameInput.addEventListener("input",
function() {
    if (usernameInput.value.trim() === "") {
        usernameError.textContent = "Username is
required";
        usernameError.style.color = "red";
    } else {
        usernameError.textContent = "";
    }
});
```

Here, we listen for the **input** event, which is triggered each time the user types. If the username field is empty, an error message is displayed dynamically.

Real-World Example: Creating a Dynamic Registration Form

Now, let's apply our knowledge and build a **dynamic registration form**. This form will include **real-time validation** for all fields, and upon form submission, it will display a summary of the user's input (instead of submitting it to a server).

Step 1: HTML Structure

Here's the structure for our dynamic registration form:

html

```
<!DOCTYPE html>
<html lang="en">
<head>
    <meta charset="UTF-8">
    <meta name="viewport" content="width=device-
width, initial-scale=1.0">
    <title>Registration Form</title>
    <style>
        .error { color: red; font-size: 0.9em; }
    </style>
</head>
<body>

<h1>Registration Form</h1>

<form id="registrationForm">
    <label for="username">Username:</label>
    <input        type="text"        id="username"
name="username" required>
    <span                    id="usernameError"
class="error"></span><br><br>

    <label for="email">Email:</label>
```

```
    <input type="email" id="email" name="email"
required>
    <span                            id="emailError"
class="error"></span><br><br>

    <label for="password">Password:</label>
    <input     type="password"     id="password"
name="password" required>
    <span                         id="passwordError"
class="error"></span><br><br>

    <button type="submit">Submit</button>
</form>

<div id="summary"></div>

<script src="script.js"></script>

</body>
</html>
```

Step 2: JavaScript for Validation and Dynamic Feedback

Here's how we can handle form validation and provide dynamic feedback for the form fields:

javascript

```
// script.js
```

```javascript
const                   form                =
document.getElementById("registrationForm");
const             usernameInput             =
document.getElementById("username");
const              emailInput               =
document.getElementById("email");
const             passwordInput             =
document.getElementById("password");

const             usernameError             =
document.getElementById("usernameError");
const              emailError               =
document.getElementById("emailError");
const             passwordError             =
document.getElementById("passwordError");
const              summaryDiv               =
document.getElementById("summary");

form.addEventListener("submit",  function(event)
{
    event.preventDefault();  // Prevent  default
form submission

    let isValid = true;
    summaryDiv.innerHTML = "";  // Clear previous
summary

    // Validate Username
    if (usernameInput.value.trim() === "") {
```

```javascript
        isValid = false;
        usernameError.textContent = "Username is
required.";
    } else {
        usernameError.textContent = "";
    }


    // Validate Email
    const emailRegex = /^[a-zA-Z0-9._-]+@[a-zA-
Z0-9.-]+\.[a-zA-Z]{2,6}$/;
    if (!emailRegex.test(emailInput.value)) {
        isValid = false;
        emailError.textContent = "Please enter a
valid email address.";
    } else {
        emailError.textContent = "";
    }


    // Validate Password
    if (passwordInput.value.length < 6) {
        isValid = false;
        passwordError.textContent  =  "Password
must be at least 6 characters long.";
    } else {
        passwordError.textContent = "";
    }


    if (isValid) {
```

```
        // If form is valid, display the user
input
        summaryDiv.innerHTML = `
            <h3>Registration Summary:</h3>
            <p>Username:
${usernameInput.value}</p>
            <p>Email: ${emailInput.value}</p>
            <p>Password:
${passwordInput.value}</p>
            `;
    }
});


// Real-time validation for username
usernameInput.addEventListener("input",
function() {
    if (usernameInput.value.trim() === "") {
        usernameError.textContent = "Username is
required.";
    } else {
        usernameError.textContent = "";
    }
});


// Real-time validation for email
emailInput.addEventListener("input", function()
{
    const emailRegex = /^[a-zA-Z0-9._-]+@[a-zA-
Z0-9.-]+\.[a-zA-Z]{2,6}$/;
```

```
    if (!emailRegex.test(emailInput.value)) {
        emailError.textContent = "Please enter a
valid email address.";
    } else {
        emailError.textContent = "";
    }
});

// Real-time validation for password
passwordInput.addEventListener("input",
function() {
    if (passwordInput.value.length < 6) {
        passwordError.textContent   =   "Password
must be at least 6 characters long.";
    } else {
        passwordError.textContent = "";
    }
});
```

Explanation:

1. **HTML**:
   - We have a basic form with **username**, **email**, and **password** fields.
   - **Error messages** are displayed below each input field if validation fails.
   - **A `summary` div** will display the form data if the form is successfully submitted.
2. **JavaScript**:

- o **Event Listener for Form Submission**: The form listens for the `submit` event, and we prevent the default submission to handle validation first.
- o **Validation**: We check if the fields are valid:
  - **Username**: Required field.
  - **Email**: Valid email pattern using a regular expression.
  - **Password**: Minimum length of 6 characters.
- o **Dynamic Feedback**: If any field is invalid, an error message is displayed under the respective field. If all fields are valid, a summary of the entered data is displayed.

Conclusion

In this chapter, we:

- Learned how to handle **form submissions** using JavaScript, including using `event.preventDefault()` to stop the default form submission.
- Implemented **dynamic form validation**, both in real-time (while typing) and when submitting the form.

- Built a **dynamic registration form** that validates the user input and provides immediate feedback.

By mastering form handling and validation, you can ensure that users interact with your web applications in a meaningful and efficient way. In the next chapter, we will explore **advanced JavaScript topics** such as **working with APIs** and **asynchronous operations**.

CHAPTER 15

INTRODUCTION TO JAVASCRIPT LIBRARIES: JQUERY AND BEYOND

JavaScript libraries provide pre-written code that allows developers to perform common tasks more efficiently. They abstract complex functionality into easy-to-use functions and save you time by reducing the amount of code you need to write. In this chapter, we will discuss **why you should use libraries like jQuery**, explore **commonly used libraries** for various tasks, and walk through a **real-world example** of creating a **slider carousel** using **jQuery**.

Why Use Libraries Like jQuery?

JavaScript libraries like **jQuery** were developed to make it easier for developers to interact with the DOM, handle events, and perform animations or AJAX requests without having to write a lot of code. Here are some reasons why libraries like jQuery are so useful:

1. **Simplified Syntax**: jQuery provides a much simpler and shorter syntax for many common JavaScript tasks, such as selecting elements, handling events, or making AJAX requests.

    For example, instead of using `document.getElementById()` and adding event listeners manually, jQuery allows you to use simple methods like `$("#element")` and `.click()`.

2. **Cross-Browser Compatibility**: One of the major challenges in web development is making sure that your website works across different browsers (e.g., Chrome, Firefox, Safari, etc.). jQuery handles these compatibility issues for you, ensuring that your code runs smoothly on all major browsers.

3. **Faster Development**: jQuery and other libraries abstract away many of the complex details of JavaScript, which makes development faster. You can focus more on your application's functionality instead of reinventing the wheel for basic tasks.

4. **Rich Ecosystem**: Libraries like jQuery have a large number of plugins and extensions that can add functionality (e.g., image sliders, pop-up modals, form validation) with minimal effort.

Commonly Used Libraries for Common Tasks

There are many JavaScript libraries available that cater to specific tasks. Here are some of the most popular ones:

1. **jQuery**:
   - **Purpose**: DOM manipulation, event handling, AJAX requests, animations, and more.
   - **Usage**: It's ideal for projects that need a lot of DOM manipulation or want to ensure cross-browser compatibility.

2. **Lodash**:
   - **Purpose**: A utility library that helps with common tasks like working with arrays, objects, and functions.
   - **Usage**: Useful for operations like deep cloning objects, manipulating arrays, or debouncing events.

3. **Axios**:
   - **Purpose**: A library for making HTTP requests.
   - **Usage**: Ideal for interacting with RESTful APIs or handling AJAX requests.

4. **Moment.js** (Deprecated in favor of newer libraries like `date-fns`):
   - **Purpose**: Date and time manipulation.
   - **Usage**: Useful for formatting, parsing, and manipulating dates and times.

5. **Chart.js**:

   o **Purpose**: Simple library for creating interactive and animated charts.

   o **Usage**: Great for displaying data visualizations on a web page.

6. **SweetAlert2**:

   o **Purpose**: Beautiful, customizable pop-up alerts.

   o **Usage**: Ideal for showing friendly, customizable alerts or confirmations.

7. **GreenSock (GSAP)**:

   o **Purpose**: Advanced animation library.

   o **Usage**: For creating high-performance, complex animations on the web.

8. **Bootstrap**:

   o **Purpose**: CSS framework with built-in JavaScript components for building responsive, mobile-first web apps.

   o **Usage**: Quickly create layouts and UI components with built-in styles and behaviors.

Real-World Example: Creating a Slider Carousel Using jQuery

Now, let's put jQuery to work by building a **slider carousel**. A carousel is a popular UI component that displays multiple images or content panels that users can slide through, usually with left and right navigation buttons.

Step 1: HTML Structure

Here's a simple HTML structure for the slider carousel.

html

```
<!DOCTYPE html>
<html lang="en">
<head>
    <meta charset="UTF-8">
    <meta name="viewport" content="width=device-
width, initial-scale=1.0">
    <title>Image Slider</title>
    <link rel="stylesheet" href="styles.css">
    <script src="https://code.jquery.com/jquery-
3.6.0.min.js"></script>
</head>
<body>

<div class="slider-container">
    <button class="prev-btn">Prev</button>
    <div class="slider">
        <div class="slide active"><img
src="https://via.placeholder.com/600x400?text=I
mage+1" alt="Image 1"></div>
        <div class="slide"><img
src="https://via.placeholder.com/600x400?text=I
mage+2" alt="Image 2"></div>
```

```
        <div              class="slide"><img
src="https://via.placeholder.com/600x400?text=I
mage+3" alt="Image 3"></div>
    </div>
    <button class="next-btn">Next</button>
</div>

<script src="script.js"></script>
</body>
</html>
```

Step 2: CSS Styling

Now, let's style the slider. We'll make sure the images are aligned horizontally and that the navigation buttons are positioned correctly.

css

```
/* styles.css */
body {
    font-family: Arial, sans-serif;
}

.slider-container {
    position: relative;
    width: 600px;
    margin: 50px auto;
    overflow: hidden;
}
```

```css
.slider {
    display: flex;
    transition: transform 0.5s ease;
}

.slide {
    min-width: 100%;
    display: flex;
    justify-content: center;
    align-items: center;
}

img {
    max-width: 100%;
    display: block;
}

button {
    position: absolute;
    top: 50%;
    transform: translateY(-50%);
    background-color: rgba(0, 0, 0, 0.5);
    color: white;
    padding: 10px;
    border: none;
    cursor: pointer;
    font-size: 18px;
}
```

```
.prev-btn {
    left: 10px;
}

.next-btn {
    right: 10px;
}
```

Step 3: jQuery Functionality

Let's now use jQuery to add functionality to the slider. We'll use jQuery to make the slides move left and right when the user clicks the navigation buttons.

```javascript
// script.js

$(document).ready(function() {
    let currentIndex = 0;
    const slides = $(".slide");
    const totalSlides = slides.length;

    // Function to update the slide
    function updateSlider() {
        // Remove the 'active' class from all slides
        slides.removeClass("active");
```

```
        // Add the 'active' class to the current
slide

$(slides[currentIndex]).addClass("active");

        //  Move   the   slider   to   the   correct
position
        $(".slider").css("transform",
"translateX(" + (-currentIndex * 100) + "%)");
    }

    // Move to the next slide
    $(".next-btn").click(function() {
        currentIndex  =  (currentIndex  +  1)  %
totalSlides;
        updateSlider();
    });

    // Move to the previous slide
    $(".prev-btn").click(function() {
        currentIndex  =  (currentIndex  -  1  +
totalSlides) % totalSlides;
        updateSlider();
    });

    // Initialize the slider
    updateSlider();
});
```

Explanation of the Code:

1. **HTML**:
   - We have a `slider-container` that contains a `slider` div, which holds the `slide` divs (each containing an image).
   - Two buttons, "Prev" and "Next", allow the user to navigate through the images.

2. **CSS**:
   - The `slider-container` is set to `relative` positioning with `overflow: hidden` to hide the parts of the images that are not currently visible.
   - The `slider` uses `display: flex` to align the images horizontally. The `transition` property on the slider creates a smooth sliding effect.
   - The `slide` class is applied to each image, ensuring they each take up 100% of the width of the container.

3. **jQuery**:
   - We maintain the `currentIndex` variable, which tracks the currently active slide.
   - When the user clicks the **Next** or **Prev** button, we update `currentIndex` and adjust the transform of the `.slider` to shift the visible slide.
   - The `updateSlider` function is responsible for adding the `active` class to the current slide and

removing it from others. It also moves the
`.slider` container to the correct position using
the `transform` property.

Conclusion

In this chapter, we:

- Learned why and how to use **JavaScript libraries** like
  jQuery to simplify tasks such as DOM manipulation,
  event handling, and animations.
- Explored **commonly used libraries** for common tasks
  like data manipulation, HTTP requests, and UI
  components.
- Built a **real-world example** of a **slider carousel** using
  jQuery, where we dynamically change the slides and
  enable user navigation.

Using libraries like jQuery helps streamline development and
saves time by handling complex tasks in just a few lines of code.
In the next chapter, we will explore more advanced JavaScript

CHAPTER 16

GETTING STARTED WITH REACT.JS

React.js is one of the most popular JavaScript libraries for building user interfaces, particularly single-page applications where data changes over time. In this chapter, we'll introduce **React**, walk through the process of setting up your first React app, and explore the key concepts of **components**, **props**, and **state**. Finally, we'll apply this knowledge to build a **to-do list app** in React.

What is React? Setting Up Your First React App

React is a declarative, efficient, and flexible JavaScript library for building user interfaces. It allows developers to build complex UIs from small, reusable pieces of code called **components**. React was created by Facebook and has become one of the most widely used tools for building modern web applications.

React uses a **virtual DOM** (Document Object Model), which makes rendering faster by updating only the parts of the page that have changed. This leads to a smooth and responsive user experience.

Why Use React?

1. **Component-Based Architecture**: React apps are built from components, which can be reused and composed to build more complex UIs.

2. **Declarative Syntax**: React allows developers to describe what the UI should look like for a given state, and React takes care of updating the UI efficiently when the state changes.

3. **Unidirectional Data Flow**: Data in React flows in one direction, making it easier to track changes in the app's state and ensure that the UI reflects the latest data.

4. **Ecosystem**: React has a strong ecosystem with tools like **React Router** for navigation, **Redux** for state management, and many other libraries.

Setting Up a React App

To get started with React, you need **Node.js** and **npm (Node Package Manager)** installed on your machine. If you haven't installed them yet, go to nodejs.org and download the latest version of Node.js.

Once Node.js is installed, you can set up your first React app using **Create React App**, a tool provided by Facebook to quickly set up a new React project.

1. Open your terminal or command prompt and run the following command to install Create React App globally:

```bash

npx create-react-app my-first-react-app
```

2. Navigate to your project directory:

```bash

cd my-first-react-app
```

3. Start the development server:

```bash

npm start
```

Your app will be available at `http://localhost:3000` in your browser.

Components, Props, and State in React

In React, everything is built using **components**. Components are independent, reusable building blocks that describe part of the user interface.

1. Components

A **component** is a JavaScript function or class that returns JSX (JavaScript XML) to define the UI. React components can be either **functional components** or **class components**.

- **Functional Components**: These are simpler and the preferred way to write components in modern React.
- **Class Components**: These were traditionally used for components that needed state and lifecycle methods, but functional components with hooks have largely replaced class components.

Example of a Functional Component:

javascript

```
function MyComponent() {
    return <h1>Hello, React!</h1>;
}
```

Example of a Class Component:

javascript

```
class MyComponent extends React.Component {
    render() {
        return <h1>Hello, React!</h1>;
    }
}
```

```
}
```

2. Props (Properties)

Props are inputs to a React component. They are passed to the component by its parent, and they allow data to be passed down through the component tree. Props are **read-only** and cannot be modified within the component that receives them.

Example of using props:

```javascript

function Greeting(props) {
    return <h1>Hello, {props.name}!</h1>;
}

function App() {
    return <Greeting name="John" />;
}
```

In this example, the `Greeting` component receives a `name` prop and uses it to display a personalized greeting.

3. State

State represents the local data of a component and can be changed over time. State is **mutable**, meaning that it can be updated based on user interaction or other events. When the state changes, React automatically re-renders the component and its children.

In functional components, you can manage state using the useState hook, while class components use this.state and this.setState().

Example of State in Functional Components:

```javascript

import React, { useState } from "react";

function Counter() {
    const [count, setCount] = useState(0);

    const increment = () => setCount(count + 1);
    const decrement = () => setCount(count - 1);

    return (
        <div>
            <h1>Counter: {count}</h1>
            <button
onClick={increment}>Increase</button>
            <button
onClick={decrement}>Decrease</button>
        </div>
    );
}

function App() {
    return <Counter />;
```

```
}
```

Here, we use `useState` to create a state variable `count` and update it when the buttons are clicked.

Real-World Example: Building a To-Do List App with React

Let's apply what we've learned and create a **to-do list app** where users can add and remove tasks. This will involve using **state** to store the list of tasks and **props** to pass data between components.

Step 1: Set Up the App Structure

1. Create a new React app:

    ```bash
    npx create-react-app todo-app
    cd todo-app
    ```

2. Replace the contents of `src/App.js` with the following code:

```javascript
import React, { useState } from "react";

function TodoItem({ task, onDelete }) {
```

```
    return (
        <div className="todo-item">
            <span>{task}</span>
            <button
onClick={onDelete}>Delete</button>
        </div>
    );
}


function TodoList({ tasks, onDeleteTask }) {
    return (
        <div className="todo-list">
            {tasks.map((task, index) => (
                <TodoItem                 key={index}
task={task} onDelete={() => onDeleteTask(index)}
/>
            ))}
        </div>
    );
}


function TodoForm({ onAddTask }) {
    const [newTask, setNewTask] = useState("");

    const handleSubmit = (event) => {
        event.preventDefault();
        if (newTask.trim()) {
            onAddTask(newTask);
            setNewTask("");
```

```
        }
    };

    return (
        <form onSubmit={handleSubmit}>
            <input
                type="text"
                value={newTask}
                onChange={(e)                    =>
setNewTask(e.target.value)}
                placeholder="Enter a task"
            />
            <button          type="submit">Add
Task</button>
        </form>
    );
}

function App() {
    const [tasks, setTasks] = useState([]);

    const addTask = (task) => {
        setTasks([...tasks, task]);
    };

    const deleteTask = (index) => {
        setTasks(tasks.filter((_, i) => i !==
index));
    };
```

```
    return (
        <div className="app">
            <h1>Todo List</h1>
            <TodoForm onAddTask={addTask} />
            <TodoList                tasks={tasks}
onDeleteTask={deleteTask} />
        </div>
    );
}

export default App;
```

Step 2: Breakdown of the Code

1. **TodoItem**:
   o A functional component that displays an individual to-do item.
   o It receives a `task` prop and an `onDelete` prop (a function to delete the task).

2. **TodoList**:
   o A functional component that displays a list of to-do items.
   o It maps through the `tasks` array and renders a `TodoItem` for each task.
   o The `onDeleteTask` function is passed down from the parent (`App`) to allow task deletion.

3. **TodoForm**:

- o A functional component with a form to input new tasks.
- o It uses the `useState` hook to manage the state of the new task input.
- o When the form is submitted, the `onAddTask` function is called to add the task to the list.

4. **App**:

- o The main component that manages the `tasks` state, which stores the list of to-do items.
- o It includes `addTask` to add new tasks and `deleteTask` to remove tasks from the list.
- o It passes the `addTask` and `deleteTask` functions to the child components as props.

Step 3: Styling (Optional)

You can add some basic styles to make the app look nice. Add the following CSS to `src/App.css`:

css

```
/* App.css */
.app {
    width: 300px;
    margin: 0 auto;
    text-align: center;
}
```

```css
.todo-list {
    margin-top: 20px;
}


.todo-item {
    display: flex;
    justify-content: space-between;
    align-items: center;
    background: #f0f0f0;
    padding: 10px;
    margin: 5px 0;
    border-radius: 5px;
}

button {
    background: red;
    color: white;
    border: none;
    padding: 5px 10px;
    cursor: pointer;
}

button:hover {
    background: darkred;
}
```

Conclusion

In this chapter, we:

- **Introduced React**: A JavaScript library for building user interfaces, focusing on components, props, and state.
- **Set up a React app**: Using `create-react-app` to quickly scaffold a new React project.
- **Created a to-do list app**: Demonstrated how to manage state, pass props between components, and handle user interactions.

React's component-based architecture and its unidirectional data flow make it a powerful tool for building interactive and dynamic user interfaces. In the next chapter, we'll explore more advanced React concepts, such as **hooks, context API**, and **routing**.

194

CHAPTER 17

VUE.JS: A LIGHTWEIGHT ALTERNATIVE TO REACT

In this chapter, we will explore **Vue.js**, a progressive JavaScript framework that offers a lightweight alternative to React. Vue.js is known for its simplicity, ease of integration, and powerful features that make it ideal for building interactive UIs and single-page applications. We will cover **Vue.js key concepts**, demonstrate how to **build a simple interactive app**, and walk through a **real-world example** of building a **calculator app** using Vue.js.

Introduction to Vue.js and Its Key Concepts

Vue.js is a **progressive framework** for building UIs and single-page applications. Unlike other frameworks that require you to adopt a complete rewrite of your app, Vue is **incrementally adoptable**—you can use as much or as little of Vue as you need. It is often described as a **"reactive framework"** because it uses a data-binding system to update the UI automatically when the data changes.

Key Concepts in Vue.js:

1. **Declarative Rendering**:
   o Vue allows you to declaratively bind the UI to data using **mustache syntax** ({{ }}). Vue takes care of the DOM updates when the data changes.
   o **Example**:

   html

   ```html
   <div id="app">
       <p>{{ message }}</p>
   </div>
   <script>
       var app = new Vue({
           el: '#app',
           data: {
               message:        'Hello,
   Vue.js!'
           }
       });
   </script>
   ```

2. **Components**:
   o Like React, Vue is component-based, meaning that your app's UI is built from reusable components. Components can have their own templates, data, methods, and styles.
   o **Example**:

196

```javascript
```

```
Vue.component('my-component', {
    template: '<div>Hello from my
component!</div>'
});
```

3. **Reactive Data Binding**:

    o Vue's reactivity system automatically updates the DOM when the state of your data changes. This is achieved by Vue's **reactivity system**, where the data is observed, and any change triggers the UI to re-render.

    o **Example**:

```javascript
```

```
new Vue({
    el: '#app',
    data: {
        counter: 0
    },
    methods: {
        increment() {
            this.counter++;
        }
    }
});
```

197

4. **Directives**:

   o Vue uses **directives** (special tokens prefixed with `v-`) to bind behavior to elements. Common directives include `v-bind`, `v-if`, `v-for`, and `v-model`.

     - **v-bind**: Dynamically bind an attribute to an expression.
     - **v-if**: Conditionally render an element.
     - **v-for**: Loop through an array or object.

5. **Vue Instance**:

   o Every Vue app starts with a Vue instance. The instance links your JavaScript code to the DOM and defines the **data**, **methods**, and other properties of the application.

6. **Two-Way Data Binding**:

   o Using the `v-model` directive, Vue provides **two-way data binding**, allowing you to synchronize input fields and data automatically.

   o **Example**:

   html

   ```html
   <input v-model="message">
   <p>{{ message }}</p>
   ```

Building a Simple Interactive App with Vue

Let's set up a basic Vue app where users can input text, and the app will display the input in real-time.

Step 1: Setting Up Vue

To start using Vue, you can either include it directly in your HTML file or use Vue CLI for a more complex setup.

For simplicity, we'll include Vue via CDN in the HTML file.

html

```
<!DOCTYPE html>
<html lang="en">
<head>
    <meta charset="UTF-8">
    <meta name="viewport" content="width=device-width, initial-scale=1.0">
    <title>Vue Interactive App</title>
    <script src="https://cdn.jsdelivr.net/npm/vue@2.6.14/dist/vue.js"></script>
</head>
<body>

<div id="app">
    <h1>{{ message }}</h1>
```

```
    <input  v-model="message"  placeholder="Type
something here">
</div>

<script>
    new Vue({
        el: '#app',
        data: {
            message: 'Hello, Vue!'
        }
    });
</script>

</body>
</html>
```

Explanation:

- We've created a Vue instance with a `message` in the `data` section.
- The `v-model` directive creates two-way data binding between the input field and the `message` variable. As the user types, the `message` variable is updated automatically, and the displayed text updates in real-time.

Real-World Example: A Calculator App Using Vue.js

Now, let's build a **simple calculator app** using Vue.js. This app will allow users to input numbers and perform basic arithmetic operations like addition, subtraction, multiplication, and division.

Step 1: HTML Structure

html

```
<!DOCTYPE html>
<html lang="en">
<head>
    <meta charset="UTF-8">
    <meta name="viewport" content="width=device-width, initial-scale=1.0">
    <title>Vue Calculator</title>
    <script src="https://cdn.jsdelivr.net/npm/vue@2.6.14/dist/vue.js"></script>
    <style>
        .calculator {
            display: grid;
            grid-template-columns:      repeat(4, 1fr);
            width: 200px;
            margin: 50px auto;
        }
        button {
            padding: 20px;
```

```
            font-size: 20px;
            border: 1px solid #ccc;
            cursor: pointer;
        }
        .output {
            grid-column: span 4;
            padding: 20px;
            background-color: #f0f0f0;
            text-align: right;
            font-size: 30px;
        }
    </style>
</head>
<body>

<div id="app">
    <div class="calculator">
        <div class="output">{{ result }}</div>
        <button
@click="appendNumber(1)">1</button>
        <button
@click="appendNumber(2)">2</button>
        <button
@click="appendNumber(3)">3</button>
        <button
@click="setOperator('+')">+</button>

        <button
@click="appendNumber(4)">4</button>
```

```
        <button
@click="appendNumber(5)">5</button>
        <button
@click="appendNumber(6)">6</button>
        <button        @click="setOperator('-')">-
</button>

        <button
@click="appendNumber(7)">7</button>
        <button
@click="appendNumber(8)">8</button>
        <button
@click="appendNumber(9)">9</button>
        <button
@click="setOperator('*')">*</button>

        <button @click="clear">C</button>
        <button
@click="appendNumber(0)">0</button>
        <button @click="calculate">=</button>
        <button
@click="setOperator('/')">/</button>
    </div>
</div>

<script>
    new Vue({
        el: '#app',
        data: {
```

```javascript
            currentInput: '',
            operator: null,
            previousInput: '',
            result: ''
      },
    methods: {
        appendNumber(number) {
            this.currentInput += number;
        },
        setOperator(operator) {
            if (this.currentInput === '')
return;
            this.previousInput         =
this.currentInput;
            this.currentInput = '';
            this.operator = operator;
        },
        calculate() {
            if (this.currentInput === '' ||
this.previousInput === '') return;

            let calculation;
            switch (this.operator) {
                case '+':
                    calculation            =
parseFloat(this.previousInput)                +
parseFloat(this.currentInput);
                        break;
                case '-':
```

```
                calculation                =
parseFloat(this.previousInput)            -
parseFloat(this.currentInput);
                break;
            case '*':
                calculation                =
parseFloat(this.previousInput)            *
parseFloat(this.currentInput);
                break;
            case '/':
                calculation                =
parseFloat(this.previousInput)            /
parseFloat(this.currentInput);
                break;
            default:
                return;
        }
        this.result = calculation;
        this.previousInput = '';
        this.currentInput = '';
    },
    clear() {
        this.currentInput = '';
        this.previousInput = '';
        this.operator = null;
        this.result = '';
    }
  }
});
```

```
</script>

</body>
</html>
```

Step 2: Breakdown of the Code

1. **HTML Structure**:
   - We've set up a basic grid layout for the calculator with buttons for numbers (0-9), operations (+, -, *, /), and a `clear` button.
   - The `output` div displays the result of the calculation.

2. **Vue Data**:
   - `currentInput`: Stores the current number input by the user.
   - `previousInput`: Stores the number before the operator.
   - `operator`: Stores the selected operator (+, -, *, /).
   - `result`: Stores the result of the calculation.

3. **Vue Methods**:
   - **appendNumber()**: Adds the clicked number to `currentInput`.
   - **setOperator()**: Stores the current number and operator and clears the input for the next number.

206

- o **calculate()**: Performs the calculation based on the current operator and inputs, then displays the result.
- o **clear()**: Resets all the fields (input and result).

Conclusion

In this chapter, we:

- **Introduced Vue.js**, a lightweight, flexible JavaScript framework for building user interfaces.
- **Learned key Vue concepts** such as **components**, **reactivity**, and **data binding**.
- **Built a simple interactive app** with Vue.js, including a **calculator app** that handles basic arithmetic operations.

Vue.js offers a simpler and more approachable alternative to other frameworks like React, making it a great choice for building modern web applications. In the next chapter, we will explore **Vue Router** for adding navigation to single-page applications and **Vuex** for advanced state management.

CHAPTER 18

ANGULAR: A COMPREHENSIVE FRAMEWORK FOR LARGE-SCALE APPS

In this chapter, we will explore **Angular**, a powerful, comprehensive framework for building large-scale, complex web applications. Unlike libraries like React and Vue.js, Angular is a full-fledged framework that comes with many built-in tools for developing single-page applications (SPAs). We will cover the **basics of Angular**, learn how to **set up an Angular project**, and build a **real-world dynamic blog app** using Angular.

Angular Basics: Modules, Components, Services, and Directives

Angular is built around the concept of **modules**, **components**, **services**, and **directives**. Let's break down these fundamental building blocks of an Angular application:

1. Modules

An **Angular module** is a container for a related set of components, services, and other Angular features that can be

208

bundled together. Every Angular application has at least one module, the **root module**, which bootstraps the application.

- **Core Module**: The root module that initializes the app.
- **Feature Modules**: Group related components and services to organize your app (e.g., a `BlogModule` for blog-related features).

Example of an Angular module:

typescript

```
import { NgModule } from '@angular/core';
import { BrowserModule } from '@angular/platform-browser';
import { AppComponent } from './app.component';

@NgModule({
  declarations: [AppComponent],      // Declare components used in this module
  imports: [BrowserModule],      // Import other modules
  providers: [],                        // Provide services
  bootstrap: [AppComponent]             // Root component
})
export class AppModule { }
```

2. Components

A **component** is the fundamental building block of an Angular application. Each component has:

- **Template**: The HTML structure that the component renders.
- **CSS**: The styles for the component.
- **Class**: The business logic for the component, written in TypeScript.

Components are typically paired with a service to handle data and logic.

Example of an Angular component:

typescript

```
import { Component } from '@angular/core';

@Component({
  selector: 'app-root',
  template: `<h1>{{ title }}</h1>`,
  styleUrls: ['./app.component.css']
})
export class AppComponent {
  title = 'Hello, Angular!';
}
```

In the above example:

- `selector` defines how the component will be used in HTML (i.e., `<app-root></app-root>`).
- `template` defines the HTML structure.
- `styleUrls` links to the CSS file for styling.

3. Services

In Angular, **services** are used to handle data and business logic. Services are typically injected into components, allowing for reusable logic that can be shared across multiple components.

Example of an Angular service:

typescript

```
import { Injectable } from '@angular/core';

@Injectable({
  providedIn: 'root',   // Makes the service
available throughout the application
})
export class BlogService {
  getPosts() {
    return ['Post 1', 'Post 2', 'Post 3'];
  }
}
```

Injecting the service into a component:

```typescript
import { Component, OnInit } from
'@angular/core';
import { BlogService } from './blog.service';

@Component({
  selector: 'app-blog',
  template: `
    <ul>
      <li *ngFor="let post of posts">{{ post
}}</li>
    </ul>
  `,
})
export class BlogComponent implements OnInit {
  posts: string[] = [];

  constructor(private blogService: BlogService)
{}

  ngOnInit() {
    this.posts = this.blogService.getPosts();
  }
}
```

4. Directives

Directives are used to add behavior to DOM elements. Angular has two types of directives:

- **Structural Directives**: Change the structure of the DOM (e.g., `*ngIf`, `*ngFor`).
- **Attribute Directives**: Change the appearance or behavior of an element (e.g., `ngClass`, `ngStyle`).

Example of a structural directive (`*ngIf`):

html

```
<p *ngIf="isVisible">This paragraph is
conditionally rendered.</p>
```

Example of an attribute directive (`ngClass`):

html

```
<div [ngClass]="{ 'active': isActive }">This div
has dynamic classes.</div>
```

Setting Up an Angular Project and Building a Small App

Now that we understand the key concepts of Angular, let's create a small Angular project and build a simple **blog app**.

Step 1: Setting Up Angular CLI

The **Angular CLI** is a command-line interface tool that helps you initialize, develop, and maintain Angular applications. To install Angular CLI, run the following command:

bash

```
npm install -g @angular/cli
```

Step 2: Creating a New Angular Project

To create a new Angular project, run the following command:

bash

```
ng new my-blog-app
cd my-blog-app
```

This will create a new Angular project with all the necessary configurations.

Step 3: Starting the Development Server

To start the Angular development server, run:

bash

```
ng serve
```

214

Your app will be available at `http://localhost:4200/` in the browser.

Step 4: Creating a Simple Blog App

Now, let's create a **blog app** that displays a list of blog posts. We will create a `BlogComponent` and a `BlogService`.

1. **Create the Blog Component**:

bash

```bash
ng generate component blog
```

This will create the following files:

*   `src/app/blog/blog.component.ts`
*   `src/app/blog/blog.component.html`
*   `src/app/blog/blog.component.css`

2. **Update the Blog Component**:

Edit `blog.component.ts`:

typescript

```typescript
import { Component, OnInit } from '@angular/core';
import { BlogService } from '../blog.service';
```

```
@Component({
  selector: 'app-blog',
  templateUrl: './blog.component.html',
  styleUrls: ['./blog.component.css']
})
export class BlogComponent implements OnInit {
  posts: string[] = [];

  constructor(private blogService: BlogService)
{}

  ngOnInit(): void {
    this.posts = this.blogService.getPosts();
  }
}
```

Edit `blog.component.html` to display the blog posts:

html

```
<h2>Blog Posts</h2>
<ul>
  <li *ngFor="let post of posts">{{ post }}</li>
</ul>
```

3. **Create the Blog Service**:

Generate the `BlogService`:

bash

```
ng generate service blog
```

Update the `blog.service.ts`:

```typescript
import { Injectable } from '@angular/core';

@Injectable({
  providedIn: 'root'
})
export class BlogService {
  getPosts(): string[] {
    return ['Post 1', 'Post 2', 'Post 3'];
  }
}
```

4. Update the Root Component (App Component):

To display the `BlogComponent`, open `app.component.html` and add:

```html
<app-blog></app-blog>
```

Real-World Example: A Dynamic Blog App Using Angular

We now have a simple **blog app** that dynamically fetches blog posts from a service and displays them in a list. The app uses:

- **Components**: `AppComponent` (root component) and `BlogComponent` (for displaying the blog posts).
- **Service**: `BlogService` for fetching blog data.
- **Directives**: `*ngFor` to loop through the blog posts and display them.

Running the Blog App

Once you've made the changes, run the app with `ng serve` and navigate to `http://localhost:4200/`. You should see a list of blog posts rendered by the `BlogComponent`.

Conclusion

In this chapter, we:

- **Introduced Angular**, a comprehensive framework for building large-scale applications with modules, components, services, and directives.
- **Set up an Angular project** using Angular CLI and created a simple blog app.

- **Built a dynamic blog app** using Angular's component-based architecture and services.

Angular's full-fledged framework approach is ideal for building complex, enterprise-level applications. In the next chapter, we will explore **Angular routing**, enabling you to navigate between pages in a single-page application.

CHAPTER 19

JAVASCRIPT DESIGN PATTERNS

In this chapter, we will explore **JavaScript design patterns**. Design patterns are general, reusable solutions to common problems in software design. They provide a way to structure your code so that it is more maintainable, reusable, and scalable. JavaScript, like other programming languages, also benefits from various design patterns, which help developers tackle issues related to object creation, data management, and behavior.

We will cover:

1. **What design patterns are and why they are important** in programming.
2. **Common design patterns** used in JavaScript development, such as the **Singleton**, **Factory**, and **Module** patterns.
3. **A real-world example** of implementing the **Singleton pattern** in a web app.

What are Design Patterns in Programming?

Design patterns are **time-tested solutions** to common problems that developers encounter when designing software. They are not code templates but rather guidelines that describe how to solve specific problems in different situations.

Design patterns help to:

- **Improve code readability**: By using a common approach, developers can understand the structure and design of code quickly.
- **Increase reusability**: Well-implemented patterns can be reused across different projects.
- **Enhance maintainability**: Design patterns make it easier to manage and extend software.

Design patterns are classified into **creational**, **structural**, and **behavioral** patterns:

- **Creational** patterns: Deal with object creation mechanisms, trying to create objects in a manner suitable to the situation (e.g., Singleton, Factory).
- **Structural** patterns: Concern how classes and objects are composed to form larger structures (e.g., Module, Adapter).
- **Behavioral** patterns: Focus on communication between objects (e.g., Observer, Strategy).

In JavaScript, we often use **creational** and **structural** patterns as they help with the management of objects and functions in a more efficient way.

Common Design Patterns in JavaScript

1. Singleton Pattern

The **Singleton pattern** ensures that a class has only one instance and provides a global point of access to that instance. This is particularly useful when we need to manage shared resources like a configuration object, a database connection, or a logging service.

The Singleton pattern ensures that only one instance of the object exists throughout the application lifecycle.

Example Use Case:

- A logging system where you want only one instance to log messages across the entire application.
- A configuration object that manages global settings for an app.

Implementation of the Singleton Pattern:

```javascript
class Singleton {
    constructor() {
        if (!Singleton.instance) {
            this.name = "Singleton Instance";
            Singleton.instance = this;
```

```
        }
        return Singleton.instance;
    }

    getName() {
        return this.name;
    }
}

// Usage
const singleton1 = new Singleton();
console.log(singleton1.getName());   // Outputs:
Singleton Instance

const singleton2 = new Singleton();
console.log(singleton2.getName());   // Outputs:
Singleton Instance

// Both instances are the same
console.log(singleton1 === singleton2);   //
Outputs: true
```

Explanation:

- **Singleton.instance** stores the first instance of the class.
- Any subsequent instantiation of the Singleton class returns the **same instance**, ensuring there is only one instance.

2. Factory Pattern

The **Factory pattern** provides an interface for creating objects in a super class, but allows subclasses to alter the type of objects that will be created. It's useful when you want to create different types of objects based on certain conditions without exposing the instantiation logic to the client.

Example Use Case:

- Creating different types of notifications (e.g., email, SMS, push notifications) based on user preferences.
- Creating different shapes (e.g., circle, square, triangle) dynamically based on user input.

Implementation of the Factory Pattern:

```javascript
class Shape {
    draw() {
        throw new Error("This method should be overridden!");
    }
}

class Circle extends Shape {
    draw() {
        console.log("Drawing a Circle");
```

```
    }
}

class Square extends Shape {
    draw() {
        console.log("Drawing a Square");
    }
}

class ShapeFactory {
    static createShape(type) {
        if (type === "circle") {
            return new Circle();
        } else if (type === "square") {
            return new Square();
        } else {
            throw    new    Error("Invalid    shape
type");
        }
    }
}

// Usage
const              circle              =
ShapeFactory.createShape("circle");
circle.draw();  // Outputs: Drawing a Circle

const              square              =
ShapeFactory.createShape("square");
```

```
square.draw();  // Outputs: Drawing a Square
```

Explanation:

- The **Shape** class is a base class with a `draw()` method.
- The **Circle** and **Square** classes extend the **Shape** class and implement the `draw()` method.
- The **ShapeFactory** class provides a `createShape()` method that returns instances of different shape classes based on the input.

3. Module Pattern

The **Module pattern** is used to encapsulate functionality in a single unit and expose only the methods that need to be accessible to the outside world. It helps keep your codebase organized by preventing global scope pollution and reducing naming conflicts.

Example Use Case:

- Creating a utility library with private methods and exposing only the necessary functions.
- Organizing application logic into modules, like user authentication, notifications, and settings.

Implementation of the Module Pattern:

```
javascript
```

```javascript
const Calculator = (function() {
    let result = 0;

    // Private method
    function add(x, y) {
        result = x + y;
    }

    function subtract(x, y) {
        result = x - y;
    }

    // Public methods
    return {
        addNumbers: function(x, y) {
            add(x, y);
            return result;
        },
        subtractNumbers: function(x, y) {
            subtract(x, y);
            return result;
        }
    };
})();

// Usage
console.log(Calculator.addNumbers(5, 3));    // Outputs: 8
```

```
console.log(Calculator.subtractNumbers(10,   4));
// Outputs: 6
```

Explanation:

- The **Calculator** module encapsulates the private `add` and `subtract` methods.
- Only the public methods `addNumbers` and `subtractNumbers` are exposed to the outside world, providing controlled access to the internal logic.
- The private variables and methods inside the module cannot be accessed directly from outside, preventing external code from altering them.

Real-World Example: Implementing a Singleton Pattern in a Web App

Let's now implement the **Singleton pattern** in a simple web app to manage a **configuration object**. We will create a `ConfigService` that holds the configuration settings for the app. The service will ensure that only one instance of the configuration object exists.

Step 1: Creating the Singleton ConfigService
javascript

```
class ConfigService {
```

```
    constructor() {
        if (!ConfigService.instance) {
            this.config = {
                apiUrl:
'https://api.example.com',
                theme: 'light',
                language: 'en'
            };
            ConfigService.instance = this;
        }
        return ConfigService.instance;
    }

    getConfig() {
        return this.config;
    }

    updateConfig(newConfig) {
        this.config    =    {    ...this.config,
...newConfig };
    }
}


// Usage
const configService1 = new ConfigService();
console.log(configService1.getConfig());       //
Outputs the config object

const configService2 = new ConfigService();
```

```javascript
configService2.updateConfig({ theme: 'dark' });
```

```javascript
console.log(configService1.getConfig());        //
Outputs updated config with 'dark' theme
console.log(configService1 === configService2);
// Outputs: true
```

Step 2: Using ConfigService in a Web App

Now that we have a `ConfigService` Singleton, we can use it to manage configuration settings in the app, ensuring that every part of the app uses the same configuration instance.

javascript

```javascript
// Example of using ConfigService in an app

const           themeButton          =
document.getElementById("theme-button");

themeButton.addEventListener("click", () => {
    const configService = new ConfigService();
    const           currentConfig          =
configService.getConfig();
    const  newTheme  =  currentConfig.theme  ===
'light' ? 'dark' : 'light';
    configService.updateConfig({ theme: newTheme
});

    document.body.className = newTheme;
```

```
    alert(`Theme changed to ${newTheme}`);
});
```

In this simple web app:

- The **Singleton pattern** ensures that there is only one `ConfigService` instance responsible for managing the configuration.
- The **theme** setting is stored in the Singleton, and changes to it are reflected globally across the app.

Conclusion

In this chapter, we:

- **Introduced JavaScript design patterns**, including **Singleton**, **Factory**, and **Module**.
- Explored how these patterns help in structuring and organizing code for maintainability and scalability.
- Implemented a **real-world Singleton pattern** to manage a configuration service in a web app.

Design patterns are valuable tools for writing clean, efficient, and maintainable code. In the next chapter, we will explore **advanced JavaScript topics** like **asynchronous programming** and **performance optimization**.

CHAPTER 20

TESTING AND DEBUGGING JAVASCRIPT CODE

In this chapter, we will explore **testing and debugging** in JavaScript, focusing on tools and practices that ensure your code is reliable and bug-free. We'll cover **unit testing** with popular testing frameworks like **Jest** and **Mocha**, dive into **Test-Driven Development (TDD)**, and conclude with a **real-world example** of writing tests for a simple JavaScript function.

What is Unit Testing?

Unit testing involves testing individual units or components of your code (typically functions or methods) in isolation from the rest of the application. The goal is to ensure that each part of the code functions correctly on its own.

Benefits of Unit Testing:

1. **Detect Bugs Early**: Unit tests help catch bugs early by testing small units of code.

2. **Simplifies Refactoring**: Having a test suite makes it safer and easier to refactor code, knowing that tests will confirm functionality remains intact.

3. **Improves Code Quality**: Writing tests forces developers to write better-structured, more maintainable code.

Unit testing frameworks like **Jest** and **Mocha** provide tools to run tests, set up expectations, and assert that the code behaves as expected.

Unit Testing with Jest and Mocha

1. Jest

Jest is a popular JavaScript testing framework developed by Facebook. It is designed to work out of the box with minimal configuration and has built-in features like assertion libraries, test runners, and mocking capabilities.

Setting Up Jest

To get started with Jest, you need to install it in your project. If you're using **npm**:

bash

```
npm install --save-dev jest
```

In your `package.json`, add a test script to run Jest:

```json
"scripts": {
    "test": "jest"
}
```

Now, you can create your first test. Let's say you have a function that adds two numbers:

```javascript
// sum.js
function sum(a, b) {
    return a + b;
}
module.exports = sum;
```

Now, let's write a test for this function:

```javascript
// sum.test.js
const sum = require('./sum');

test('adds 1 + 2 to equal 3', () => {
    expect(sum(1, 2)).toBe(3);
});
```

Running the Test

In your terminal, run the following command:

```bash
bash
```

```
npm test
```

Jest will automatically detect the `.test.js` files and run the tests. The result should show that the test passed.

---

2. Mocha

Mocha is another popular JavaScript testing framework. Unlike Jest, Mocha is focused on the test runner, and you typically need to pair it with an assertion library like **Chai**.

Setting Up Mocha

To install Mocha, use:

```bash
bash
```

```
npm install --save-dev mocha chai
```

In your `package.json`, add a test script to run Mocha:

```json
json
```

```
"scripts": {
    "test": "mocha"
}
```

Writing Tests with Mocha and Chai

Let's use the same sum function and write a test using Mocha and Chai:

javascript

```javascript
// sum.js
function sum(a, b) {
    return a + b;
}
module.exports = sum;
```

javascript

```javascript
// test/sum.test.js
const chai = require('chai');
const sum = require('../sum');
const expect = chai.expect;

describe('sum', () => {
    it('should add 1 and 2 to get 3', () => {
        expect(sum(1, 2)).to.equal(3);
    });
});
```

Running the Mocha Test

To run the test, use:

```bash
```

```
npm test
```

Mocha will execute the test and report the result.

Test-Driven Development (TDD) in JavaScript

Test-Driven Development (TDD) is a software development practice where you write **tests before** you write the actual code. The cycle is known as **Red-Green-Refactor**:

1. **Red**: Write a test that fails (since the functionality isn't implemented yet).
2. **Green**: Write the minimal code to pass the test.
3. **Refactor**: Clean up the code, keeping the test green.

This approach helps ensure that the code you write is fully tested and that all functionality is accounted for.

TDD Example: Writing a Calculator Function

Let's use TDD to create a simple calculator function that adds two numbers.

1. **Write the Test First**:

javascript

```javascript
// calculator.test.js
const calculator = require('./calculator');

test('adds 1 + 2 to equal 3', () => {
    expect(calculator.add(1, 2)).toBe(3);
});
```

2. **Write the Code to Pass the Test**:

javascript

```javascript
// calculator.js
function add(a, b) {
    return a + b;
}

module.exports = { add };
```

3. **Run the Test**:

bash

```bash
npm test
```

The test should pass because the function correctly adds the numbers.

4. **Refactor the Code**:

In this simple example, the code is already minimal, so no refactoring is needed. But in larger projects, this phase allows you to clean up the code without affecting its functionality.

Real-World Example: Writing Tests for a Simple Function

Let's create a function that validates email addresses. We will write tests for this function using **Jest** and then implement the function to pass the tests.

Step 1: Writing the Test for Email Validation
javascript

```javascript
// emailValidator.test.js
const emailValidator = require('./emailValidator');

test('validates valid email addresses', () => {

expect(emailValidator('test@example.com')).toBe(true);

expect(emailValidator('user.name@domain.co')).toBe(true);
});
```

```
test('invalidates invalid email addresses', () =>
{

expect(emailValidator('plainaddress')).toBe(fal
se);

expect(emailValidator('missing@domain')).toBe(f
alse);
});
```

Step 2: Writing the Email Validation Function

```javascript
// emailValidator.js
function emailValidator(email) {
    const regex = /^[a-zA-Z0-9._-]+@[a-zA-Z0-9.-
]+\.[a-zA-Z]{2,6}$/;
    return regex.test(email);
}

module.exports = emailValidator;
```

Step 3: Running the Tests

To run the tests, use the following command:

```bash
npm test
```

Jest will execute the tests, and since the function correctly validates email addresses, all tests should pass.

Conclusion

In this chapter, we:

- **Explored unit testing** in JavaScript, using tools like **Jest** and **Mocha** to write and run tests.
- Learned about **Test-Driven Development (TDD)** and practiced writing tests before implementing code to ensure our software works as expected.
- Worked through a **real-world example** by writing tests for a simple email validation function and implementing the function to pass those tests.

Testing your JavaScript code is essential for ensuring that your applications are reliable, maintainable, and bug-free. In the next chapter, we will dive into **debugging techniques** and tools to help you identify and fix issues more efficiently in your code.

CHAPTER 21

JAVASCRIPT PERFORMANCE OPTIMIZATION

Performance is critical in web development. As users expect faster and more responsive applications, optimizing JavaScript code to load quickly and run efficiently is essential. In this chapter, we will cover **best practices** for **optimizing JavaScript performance**, including **lazy loading**, **code splitting**, and strategies for **identifying and fixing bottlenecks**. We will also walk through a **real-world example** of optimizing an image gallery app.

Tips for Improving JavaScript Performance

1. Lazy Loading

Lazy loading is a technique used to delay loading certain resources or components until they are needed. This reduces the initial load time of the page and improves the performance of your application.

For example, you can **lazy load images**, JavaScript modules, or other assets only when they become visible in the viewport or when they are required for functionality.

Lazy loading images:

html

```
<img src="image.jpg" alt="Image" loading="lazy">
```

- The `loading="lazy"` attribute tells the browser to load the image only when it is about to enter the viewport, reducing unnecessary network requests and improving page load times.

Lazy loading JavaScript with `import()`:

javascript

```
function loadComponent() {
    import('./component.js').then(module => {
        // Use the dynamically imported module
        const         component        =        new
module.Component();
        component.render();
    });
}
```

- **Dynamic imports** allow you to load JavaScript modules only when they are needed, thus reducing the amount of JavaScript that needs to be initially loaded.

2. Code Splitting

Code splitting is a technique used to split your JavaScript bundle into smaller files (or "chunks") that can be loaded as needed. This helps in reducing the initial load time by only loading the necessary code for the current page or route.

Code splitting with Webpack:

javascript

```
// Assuming you're using Webpack
import(/* webpackChunkName: "myComponent" */
'./myComponent.js')
    .then(module => {
        // Use the dynamically loaded module
        const         myComponent         =         new
module.MyComponent();
        myComponent.render();
    });
```

- Webpack supports **dynamic imports** that allow you to split your code into smaller chunks based on the application's needs.

3. Minification and Compression

Minification and **compression** reduce the size of your JavaScript files, leading to faster download times.

244

- **Minification**: Removes unnecessary whitespace, comments, and renames variables to reduce file size.
- **Compression**: Uses algorithms like **gzip** or **Brotli** to compress JavaScript files on the server, which are then decompressed by the browser.

You can use tools like **Terser** or Webpack's `TerserWebpackPlugin` for JavaScript minification and use server-side tools (like **Gzip** or **Brotli**) to compress files.

4. Reduce DOM Manipulation

Frequent DOM manipulation can slow down your web application because it causes the browser to reflow and repaint parts of the page. To improve performance, minimize direct manipulation of the DOM and **batch DOM updates** together.

Instead of making several DOM changes one by one, make them all in one go:

javascript

```javascript
// Inefficient way:
element.style.backgroundColor = "red";
element.style.color = "blue";

// Efficient way:
element.style.cssText = "background-color: red;
color: blue;";
```

Another best practice is to use **document fragments** to build elements in memory before inserting them into the DOM.

javascript

```
const                    fragment                =
document.createDocumentFragment();
const listItem = document.createElement("li");
listItem.textContent = "New Item";
fragment.appendChild(listItem);
document.querySelector("ul").appendChild(fragme
nt);
```

5. Debouncing and Throttling

For events that fire frequently (like `resize`, `scroll`, or `input`), use **debouncing** or **throttling** to limit the number of function calls.

- **Debouncing** ensures that a function is only called after a certain amount of idle time (e.g., after the user stops typing).
- **Throttling** limits the number of times a function can be called within a certain period (e.g., limiting how often a function is called during scrolling).

Example of debouncing:

javascript

```
let timer;
function debounce(func, delay) {
    return function(...args) {
        clearTimeout(timer);
        timer = setTimeout(() => func(...args),
delay);
    };
}

const search = debounce(function(event) {
    console.log("Search                query:",
event.target.value);
}, 300);

document.getElementById("search").addEventListe
ner("input", search);
```

Identifying and Fixing Bottlenecks

Performance bottlenecks can occur for many reasons, and identifying them requires careful analysis. Here are a few strategies to diagnose and fix performance issues in your JavaScript code:

1. Profiling with Browser DevTools

Modern browsers provide powerful **Developer Tools** (DevTools) that include a **Performance Profiler** for analyzing the performance of your web app.

- **Use the Performance tab** in Chrome DevTools to record and analyze the runtime of your JavaScript code.
- Look for long-running tasks, excessive reflows, and high CPU usage.
- The **Memory** tab helps identify memory leaks and excessive memory usage, especially in long-running apps.

2. Identifying Slow Functions with `console.time()`

You can use `console.time()` and `console.timeEnd()` to measure how long a specific piece of code takes to execute.

```javascript
console.time("myFunction");
myFunction();
console.timeEnd("myFunction");
```

If a function is taking too long to execute, consider optimizing its algorithm or breaking it up into smaller chunks.

3. Reducing JavaScript Bundles

Large JavaScript bundles can slow down your page load time. You can analyze and reduce the size of your bundles by:

- Using **Webpack Bundle Analyzer** to visualize the content of your bundles and identify large dependencies.
- Implementing **tree shaking** to remove unused code.
- Using **lazy loading** to load parts of your app only when they are needed.

Real-World Example: Optimizing an Image Gallery App for Performance

Imagine you are working on an **image gallery app** where users can view and navigate through a large number of images. This app could experience performance issues if all images are loaded at once, especially if there are hundreds or thousands of images.

Step 1: Implementing Lazy Loading for Images

To optimize the app's performance, you can implement **lazy loading** for the images. This will ensure that images are only loaded when they are about to be visible in the viewport.

html

```
<img      src="image1.jpg"      alt="Image      1"
loading="lazy">
<img      src="image2.jpg"      alt="Image      2"
loading="lazy">
<!-- More images -->
```

By adding the `loading="lazy"` attribute to each image, the browser will only load the image when it's about to be shown, significantly improving the page's load time.

Step 2: Code Splitting and Lazy Loading JavaScript

Instead of loading the entire JavaScript bundle upfront, you can **split** the code into smaller chunks that are loaded only when needed (e.g., when the user navigates to a particular section of the gallery).

In modern build tools like **Webpack**, this is done automatically when you use **dynamic imports**.

javascript

```javascript
// Lazy load the gallery component
import(/*    webpackChunkName:    "gallery"    */
'./gallery').then(module => {
    const Gallery = module.default;
    new Gallery().init();
});
```

This way, the gallery component and its associated JavaScript code are only loaded when the user interacts with the gallery section, reducing the initial load time.

Step 3: Optimizing Image Size

For an image gallery app, optimizing the image size can greatly reduce the loading time. You can serve **smaller versions of images** (thumbnails) and load the full-size images only when required, such as when the user clicks on an image.

Example: Use the `srcset` attribute to serve responsive images that load different sizes based on the screen resolution.

html

```
<img src="image-small.jpg"
    srcset="image-medium.jpg    600w,    image-
large.jpg 1200w"
    alt="Image Gallery"
    loading="lazy">
```

This approach ensures that users on lower-resolution devices load smaller images, while users on high-resolution devices load high-quality images.

Conclusion

In this chapter, we:

- Explored **performance optimization techniques** such as **lazy loading**, **code splitting**, and **minification** to reduce load time and improve responsiveness.
- Learned how to identify and fix **performance bottlenecks** using **DevTools**, **console timers**, and **profiling**.
- Worked through a **real-world example** by optimizing an **image gallery app** using lazy loading, code splitting, and image optimization.

Performance optimization is an essential skill for modern web development, ensuring that users experience fast and responsive applications. In the next chapter, we will explore **advanced JavaScript topics** related to **web security** and **best practices for safe coding**.

CHAPTER 22

SECURITY BEST PRACTICES IN JAVASCRIPT

Security is a critical aspect of web development, and ensuring that your JavaScript code is secure is essential for protecting both your users and your application from malicious attacks. In this chapter, we will focus on **securing your web app** from common vulnerabilities such as **Cross-Site Scripting (XSS)** and **Cross-Site Request Forgery (CSRF)**. We will also discuss how to use **HTTPS, Content Security Policies (CSP)**, and implement **secure coding practices**. Finally, we will walk through a **real-world example** of protecting form data with **proper validation**.

Securing Your Web App from Common Vulnerabilities

1. Cross-Site Scripting (XSS)

XSS is a vulnerability that allows attackers to inject malicious scripts into webpages viewed by other users. These scripts can steal sensitive information, such as session cookies or personal data, and perform malicious actions on behalf of users.

Preventing XSS:

- **Escape user input**: Always escape user input to prevent it from being treated as code.
- **Use libraries and frameworks**: Modern libraries like **React** automatically escape content rendered from user inputs, reducing the risk of XSS.
- **Sanitize user input**: Use libraries like **DOMPurify** to sanitize input and remove malicious scripts.

Example of XSS vulnerability:

html

```
<!-- Unsafe HTML rendering -->
<div id="output"></div>
<script>
    const    userInput    =    '<img    src="x"
onerror="alert(\'XSS Attack!\')">';
    document.getElementById("output").innerHTML
= userInput;
</script>
```

In this case, the user input is directly inserted into the HTML using `innerHTML`, which can lead to **XSS** if the input contains a malicious script.

Secure solution:

javascript

```
// Safe HTML rendering using textContent
document.getElementById("output").textContent =
userInput;
```

By using `textContent`, the input is treated as plain text, and the malicious script will not be executed.

2. Cross-Site Request Forgery (CSRF)

CSRF is an attack where a malicious user can trick a victim into performing actions they didn't intend, such as making an unwanted request on a website where the user is authenticated. For example, a CSRF attack might cause a user to unknowingly transfer money from their bank account.

Preventing CSRF:

- **Use Anti-CSRF Tokens**: Generate a unique token for each request and verify that the token matches the expected value. This prevents attackers from making unauthorized requests.
- **SameSite Cookies**: Set the `SameSite` attribute to **Strict** or **Lax** for cookies, which prevents cookies from being sent with cross-site requests.

Example of CSRF vulnerability:

```
html
```

```html
<!-- Malicious website -->
<form       action="https://example.com/transfer"
method="POST">
    <input      type="hidden"      name="amount"
value="1000">
    <input type="submit" value="Transfer Money">
</form>
```

An attacker might trick a user into submitting this form by embedding it in a malicious website, leading to an unintended money transfer.

Preventing CSRF:

html

```html
<!-- Example of a form with an anti-CSRF token -
->
<form action="/submit" method="POST">
    <input      type="hidden"      name="csrf_token"
value="{{csrf_token}}">
    <input type="text" name="message" required>
    <button type="submit">Submit</button>
</form>
```

In this case, the server should generate a **unique csrf_token** for each session, and the form should include this token in the request. When the server receives the request, it will validate the token to ensure it is legitimate.

3. Input Validation and Sanitization

Validating and sanitizing user input is an essential step in securing your application. Never trust user input without validation, and always sanitize it to ensure that it is safe to use.

- **Use regular expressions** to validate emails, phone numbers, and other input fields.
- **Sanitize input** to remove any potentially harmful characters, especially if the input will be displayed or processed in a sensitive context.

Using HTTPS, Content Security Policies, and Secure Coding Practices

1. Use HTTPS (HyperText Transfer Protocol Secure)

HTTPS encrypts data transmitted between the browser and the server, ensuring that sensitive data like passwords, credit card information, and personal details are transmitted securely. HTTPS prevents attackers from intercepting or tampering with data in transit.

- **Obtain an SSL/TLS Certificate**: You must get a certificate from a trusted certificate authority (CA) to enable HTTPS on your server.

- **Enforce HTTPS**: Redirect all HTTP traffic to HTTPS using HTTP Strict Transport Security (HSTS) headers.

```http
```

```
Strict-Transport-Security:      max-age=31536000;
includeSubDomains
```

This tells browsers to only use HTTPS for the domain for a year (`max-age=31536000`).

2. Content Security Policy (CSP)

A **Content Security Policy (CSP)** is a security mechanism that helps prevent attacks like XSS by specifying which resources (such as scripts, images, or styles) the browser is allowed to load.

- **Set a strict CSP header** to control which domains your web app can fetch resources from.

```http
```

```
Content-Security-Policy:    default-src   'self';
script-src   'self'   'https://trusted-cdn.com';
style-src 'self';
```

This policy tells the browser to only load scripts and styles from the same domain (`'self'`) or from a trusted CDN.

258

3. Secure Coding Practices

- **Use strong password hashing**: When storing passwords, always use strong hashing algorithms such as bcrypt or Argon2, not plain text.
- **Avoid using `eval()`**: The `eval()` function can execute arbitrary code, which is dangerous and often leads to vulnerabilities like XSS.
- **Principle of Least Privilege**: Limit user permissions to only what they need to perform their tasks. This helps minimize potential damage from attacks.

Real-World Example: Protecting Your Form Data with Proper Validation

Now that we've discussed how to secure web apps from common vulnerabilities, let's apply this knowledge to an actual example: a simple **contact form**.

Step 1: Frontend Form Validation

We'll start by validating the form data on the client side before it is submitted.

```html
<form id="contactForm">
```

```
    <input   type="text"   id="name"   name="name"
placeholder="Enter your name" required>
    <input  type="email"  id="email"  name="email"
placeholder="Enter your email" required>
    <textarea    id="message"    name="message"
placeholder="Enter         your        message"
required></textarea>
    <button type="submit">Submit</button>
</form>
```

Client-side validation with JavaScript:

javascript

```
document.getElementById('contactForm').addEvent
Listener('submit', function(event) {
    event.preventDefault();

    const            name               =
document.getElementById('name').value;
    const            email              =
document.getElementById('email').value;
    const            message            =
document.getElementById('message').value;

    // Validate name (must contain letters)
    if (!/^[a-zA-Z\s]+$/.test(name)) {
        alert('Name    should    only    contain
letters.');
        return;
```

```
    }

    // Validate email using regex
    const emailRegex = /^[a-zA-Z0-9._-]+@[a-zA-
Z0-9.-]+\.[a-zA-Z]{2,6}$/;
    if (!emailRegex.test(email)) {
        alert('Please    enter    a    valid    email
address.');
        return;
    }

    // Validate message (not empty)
    if (message.trim() === '') {
        alert('Message cannot be empty.');
        return;
    }

    // Proceed to submit the form (e.g., via
AJAX)
    alert('Form submitted successfully!');
});
```

In this example:

- We validate the **name**, **email**, and **message** fields before submitting the form.
- The **name** field is validated using a regular expression to allow only letters and spaces.

- The **email** field is validated using a regular expression to ensure it's in a proper email format.
- The **message** field is checked to ensure it's not empty.

Step 2: Server-Side Validation

On the server, it's crucial to **always validate and sanitize** the form data again before processing it, even though it has been validated on the client side. Never trust the data from the client!

Example in Node.js with Express:

```javascript
const express = require('express');
const app = express();
app.use(express.json());

app.post('/submit-form', (req, res) => {
    const { name, email, message } = req.body;

    // Server-side validation
    if (!/^[a-zA-Z\s]+$/.test(name)) {
        return    res.status(400).send('Invalid
name');
    }

    const emailRegex = /^[a-zA-Z0-9._-]+@[a-zA-
Z0-9.-]+\.[a-zA-Z]{2,6}$/;
```

```
    if (!emailRegex.test(email)) {
        return    res.status(400).send('Invalid
email address');
    }

    if (!message.trim()) {
        return    res.status(400).send('Message
cannot be empty');
    }

    // Process form data (e.g., save to database
or send email)
    res.send('Form submitted successfully!');
});

app.listen(3000, () => {
    console.log('Server   is   running   on   port
3000');
});
```

In this example:

- We perform **server-side validation** to ensure the name, email, and message are valid.
- **Sanitization** can also be added here to remove any potentially dangerous characters from the data.

Conclusion

In this chapter, we:

- **Secured web apps** from common vulnerabilities like **XSS** and **CSRF** by using input validation, anti-CSRF tokens, and proper escaping.
- Learned how to **use HTTPS, Content Security Policies**, and **secure coding practices** to improve the security of web applications.
- Walked through a **real-world example** of **form data validation** to protect user input from being exploited.

Securing your JavaScript application is a continuous process. By applying these security practices, you can mitigate common vulnerabilities and ensure that your web app is safe and reliable. In the next chapter, we will delve deeper into **advanced JavaScript features** and explore topics like **Web Workers** and **Service Workers**.

CHAPTER 23

WORKING WITH DATABASES IN JAVASCRIPT

In this chapter, we will explore how JavaScript interacts with **backend databases** such as **MongoDB** (NoSQL) and **SQL databases** (like MySQL or PostgreSQL). We'll also look at how to **connect** JavaScript applications to databases, manage data, and interact with it. Finally, we will walk through a **real-world example**: building a **blog application** with a **database backend**.

Introduction to Backend Databases (MongoDB and SQL)

Databases are essential for storing, retrieving, and manipulating data in a web application. There are two main types of databases you can use in modern web applications:

1. MongoDB (NoSQL Database)

MongoDB is a **NoSQL database** that stores data in **JSON-like documents** with dynamic schemas. This allows for flexible data structures and is often used when data doesn't fit well into a table-like format, such as for hierarchical or unstructured data.

- **Documents** in MongoDB are **key-value pairs**, similar to JSON objects.
- MongoDB allows for fast read and write operations and is highly scalable.

Example of a MongoDB document:

json

```
{
    "_id": "12345",
    "title": "My First Blog Post",
    "content": "This is the content of the first
post.",
    "author": "Jane Doe",
    "datePosted": "2025-04-12"
}
```

2. SQL Databases (Relational Databases)

SQL databases, such as **MySQL** or **PostgreSQL**, are **relational** databases that store data in **tables** with rows and columns. SQL (Structured Query Language) is used to interact with relational databases.

- **Tables** in SQL databases are structured with predefined columns.
- Data is related and organized in tables, and relationships between data are maintained via **foreign keys**.

266

Example of a table in SQL:

sql

```
CREATE TABLE blog_posts (
    id INT PRIMARY KEY AUTO_INCREMENT,
    title VARCHAR(255),
    content TEXT,
    author VARCHAR(100),
    datePosted DATETIME
);
```

When to Use MongoDB vs SQL?

- **MongoDB** is ideal for applications with complex, hierarchical data structures or when you need a flexible schema.
- **SQL databases** are suitable for applications that require structured data, relationships between entities, and data consistency.

How JavaScript Can Interact with Databases

JavaScript can interact with both **NoSQL** (MongoDB) and **SQL** databases via the **backend**, typically using Node.js. Here's how it works for each:

1. Interacting with MongoDB

To interact with MongoDB in JavaScript, you can use the **MongoDB Node.js Driver** or **Mongoose**, a popular ODM (Object Data Modeling) library that simplifies working with MongoDB in Node.js.

- **MongoDB Node.js Driver**: Directly interacts with the MongoDB database.
- **Mongoose**: Provides a higher-level abstraction, with schemas, models, and easy-to-use methods for interacting with MongoDB.

Example: Setting up MongoDB with Node.js

1. **Install MongoDB and Mongoose**:

   bash

   ```
   npm install mongoose
   ```

2. **Create a Mongoose Model for a Blog Post**:

   javascript

   ```
   const mongoose = require('mongoose');

   // Connect to MongoDB
   ```

```
mongoose.connect('mongodb://localhost:270
17/blogdb',    {    useNewUrlParser:    true,
useUnifiedTopology: true });

const blogSchema = new mongoose.Schema({
    title: String,
    content: String,
    author: String,
    datePosted: { type: Date, default:
Date.now }
});

const            BlogPost            =
mongoose.model('BlogPost', blogSchema);
```

3. **Save a new Blog Post**:

```javascript
const newPost = new BlogPost({
    title: 'My First Blog Post',
    content: 'This is the content of the
first post.',
    author: 'Jane Doe'
});

newPost.save((err) => {
    if (err) return console.error(err);
    console.log('Blog post saved!');
});
```

2. Interacting with SQL Databases

To interact with SQL databases, JavaScript applications use libraries such as **MySQL2**, **Sequelize**, or **pg** (for PostgreSQL).

- **MySQL2**: A MySQL client for Node.js that allows you to query and manage MySQL databases.
- **Sequelize**: An ORM (Object-Relational Mapper) for Node.js that provides an abstraction layer for SQL databases and simplifies interaction with them.

Example: Setting up MySQL with Node.js

1. **Install MySQL2**:

```bash
npm install mysql2
```

2. **Create a MySQL Connection and Query the Database**:

```javascript
const mysql = require('mysql2');

// Create a connection to the database
const connection = mysql.createConnection({
```

270

```
      host: 'localhost',
      user: 'root',
      password: 'password',
      database: 'blogdb'
});

// Query the database to fetch all blog
posts
connection.query('SELECT       *       FROM
blog_posts', (err, results) => {
    if (err) throw err;
    console.log(results);
});
```

Real-World Example: Building a Blog with a Database Backend

Now that we've seen how to interact with MongoDB and SQL databases, let's walk through the steps to build a **blog** with a **database backend**.

Step 1: Set up the Backend (Node.js + Express)

1. **Install Node.js and Express**:

    bash

    ```
    npm init -y
    npm install express mongoose
    ```

2. **Create the `server.js` file**:

```javascript
const express = require('express');
const mongoose = require('mongoose');
const app = express();

// Connect to MongoDB
mongoose.connect('mongodb://localhost:270
17/blogdb', { useNewUrlParser: true,
useUnifiedTopology: true });

// Define a schema for blog posts
const blogSchema = new mongoose.Schema({
    title: String,
    content: String,
    author: String,
    datePosted: { type: Date, default:
Date.now }
});

const BlogPost =
mongoose.model('BlogPost', blogSchema);

// Middleware to parse JSON requests
app.use(express.json());

// Create a new blog post
app.post('/posts', (req, res) => {
```

```
    const         newPost        =          new
BlogPost(req.body);
    newPost.save((err, post) => {
        if           (err)            return
res.status(500).send('Error    saving    the
post.');
        res.status(201).json(post);
    });
});


// Fetch all blog posts
app.get('/posts', (req, res) => {
    BlogPost.find({}, (err, posts) => {
        if           (err)            return
res.status(500).send('Error        fetching
posts.');
        res.status(200).json(posts);
    });
});


// Start the server
app.listen(3000, () => {
    console.log('Server       running       on
http://localhost:3000');
});
```

Step 2: Frontend to Interact with the Backend

Let's build a simple **frontend** using HTML and JavaScript to interact with the backend.

273

1. **Create the `index.html` file:**

html

```
<!DOCTYPE html>
<html lang="en">
<head>
    <meta charset="UTF-8">
    <meta                     name="viewport"
content="width=device-width,        initial-
scale=1.0">
    <title>Blog App</title>
</head>
<body>
    <h1>Blog Posts</h1>
    <div id="blogPosts"></div>

    <h2>Create a new post</h2>
    <form id="blogForm">
        <input   type="text"   id="title"
placeholder="Title" required><br>
        <textarea              id="content"
placeholder="Content"
required></textarea><br>
        <input   type="text"   id="author"
placeholder="Author" required><br>
        <button        type="submit">Create
Post</button>
    </form>
```

274

```
<script>
    // Fetch and display blog posts
    fetch('/posts')
        .then(response                  =>
response.json())
        .then(posts => {
            const    blogPostsDiv    =
document.getElementById('blogPosts');
            posts.forEach(post => {
                const postElement   =
document.createElement('div');
                postElement.innerHTML
=
`<h3>${post.title}</h3><p>${post.content}
</p><p><i>${post.author}</i></p>`;

blogPostsDiv.appendChild(postElement);
            });
        });

    // Submit a new post

document.getElementById('blogForm').addEv
entListener('submit', function (event) {
        event.preventDefault();

        const newPost = {
            title:
document.getElementById('title').value,
```

```
                content:
document.getElementById('content').value,
                author:
document.getElementById('author').value
            };

        fetch('/posts', {
            method: 'POST',
            headers: {
                'Content-Type':
'application/json'
            },
            body:
JSON.stringify(newPost)
        })
        .then(response              =>
response.json())
        .then(post => {
            console.log('Post
created:', post);
            window.location.reload();
        });
    });
  </script>
</body>
</html>
```

Step 3: Running the Application

- Start the backend server:

```bash

node server.js
```

- Open `index.html` in your browser. You can now create and display blog posts stored in your **MongoDB database**.

Conclusion

In this chapter, we:

- Explored how to work with **backend databases** like **MongoDB** and **SQL** (MySQL/PostgreSQL).
- Learned how **JavaScript can interact** with databases using **Node.js**, **Mongoose** for MongoDB, and **MySQL2** for SQL databases.
- Built a **blog application** with a database backend that allows users to create and display blog posts.

Understanding how to interact with databases is an essential skill for full-stack JavaScript development. In the next chapter, we will explore how to deploy JavaScript applications to production environments.

CHAPTER 24

DEPLOYING YOUR JAVASCRIPT APP

Deploying your JavaScript app to production is the final step in the development process. It makes your app accessible to users, allowing them to interact with it through their browsers. In this chapter, we'll go through the process of **preparing your app for production**, **hosting on popular platforms like Netlify, Heroku, and Vercel**, and walk through a **real-world example** of deploying a simple web app on **Netlify**.

Preparing Your App for Production

Before deploying your app, you need to ensure that it's optimized and ready for production. This includes the following steps:

1. Minification and Bundling

- **Minification**: Minifying your JavaScript, CSS, and HTML files reduces their size by removing unnecessary characters, such as whitespace and comments. This improves loading times.

- **Bundling**: Bundling combines multiple files (JavaScript, CSS) into one or more files, reducing the number of HTTP requests required to load your app.

Tools to minify and bundle:

- **Webpack**: A powerful module bundler that can bundle and minify JavaScript and other assets.
- **Parcel**: An easy-to-use, zero-config bundler that handles bundling and minification automatically.
- **Rollup**: A module bundler optimized for smaller libraries and applications.

bash

```
npm install --save-dev webpack webpack-cli
```

2. Environment Variables

- Set **environment variables** to differentiate between development and production environments. For example, you might have a **DATABASE_URL** that differs between local development and the production environment.

In Node.js, you can use **dotenv** to manage environment variables:

bash

```
npm install dotenv
```

279

Create a `.env` file in the root of your project:

plaintext

```
DATABASE_URL=your-production-database-url
```

In your code, use the variables:

javascript

```
require('dotenv').config();

const dbUrl = process.env.DATABASE_URL;
```

3. Optimize Assets

- **Image Optimization**: Use compressed image formats like WebP or use services like **Cloudinary** or **ImageOptim** for better image loading times.
- **Lazy Loading**: Implement lazy loading for images and JavaScript, so that only the essential parts of the page are loaded first.

4. Error Handling and Logging

- Ensure that your application handles errors gracefully. Display friendly error messages to users and log errors on the server for future troubleshooting.

In production, you can use services like **Sentry** or **LogRocket** to track and report errors in real time.

5. Security

- **Use HTTPS**: Ensure that all traffic between the client and server is encrypted using HTTPS.
- **HTTP Headers**: Set security-related HTTP headers, like `Content-Security-Policy`, `Strict-Transport-Security`, and `X-Content-Type-Options`.

Hosting on Platforms like Netlify, Heroku, and Vercel

1. Netlify

Netlify is a platform for deploying static websites and serverless functions. It provides a seamless integration with GitHub and supports automatic deployments from a Git repository. Netlify is ideal for static websites and JAMstack apps.

Deploying a Static Web App on Netlify

1. **Create a Git Repository**: If you haven't already, push your project to a Git repository (GitHub, GitLab, Bitbucket).

2. **Connect to Netlify**: Go to Netlify and sign up/log in. Then, click **"New site from Git"** and connect to your Git repository.

3. **Configure Build Settings**: For static sites, Netlify automatically detects the build settings. If you're using **React** or another build tool, specify the build command (e.g., `npm run build`) and the directory to deploy (e.g., `build/` for React apps).

4. **Deploy**: Netlify will deploy your site and give you a live URL.

---

2. Heroku

Heroku is a cloud platform that enables developers to deploy and manage applications quickly. It's widely used for full-stack JavaScript applications, especially those built with **Node.js**.

Deploying a Node.js App on Heroku

1. **Install the Heroku CLI**: Download and install the Heroku CLI.

2. **Create a Heroku App**:
   - Initialize a Git repository (if you haven't already) and commit your code.

   bash

```
git init
git add .
git commit -m "Initial commit"
```

- o   Create a new app on Heroku:

```
bash
```

```
heroku create my-node-app
```

3. **Deploy to Heroku**:
   - o   Push your code to Heroku:

```
bash
```

```
git push heroku master
```

- o   Heroku will automatically detect the environment
  (Node.js) and deploy your app.

4. **Open Your App**: Once deployed, open your app with the
   following command:

```
bash
```

```
heroku open
```

3. Vercel

Vercel is a platform for frontend deployment that works well with frameworks like **Next.js**, **React**, and other static websites. It supports serverless functions, making it a good choice for modern JavaScript applications.

Deploying a Static Web App on Vercel

1. **Create a Git Repository**: Push your app to GitHub, GitLab, or Bitbucket.
2. **Sign up for Vercel**: Go to <u>Vercel</u> and sign up or log in.
3. **Connect to Your Git Repository**: Vercel will prompt you to connect to your Git provider (GitHub, GitLab, or Bitbucket).
4. **Deploy Your App**: After selecting your repository, Vercel will automatically deploy your app. It detects the framework and deploys it accordingly.
5. **View the Deployment**: Once the deployment is complete, Vercel will provide you with a live URL.

Real-World Example: Deploying a Simple Web App on Netlify

Let's deploy a simple **static HTML/CSS/JavaScript** app on **Netlify**.

Step 1: Set Up the Project

Let's assume you have the following directory structure:

bash

```
/my-app
   /index.html
   /style.css
   /script.js
```

Step 2: Initialize a Git Repository

bash

```
cd my-app
git init
git add .
git commit -m "Initial commit"
```

Step 3: Push to GitHub

Create a repository on GitHub and push your code:

bash

```
git           remote           add           origin
https://github.com/yourusername/my-app.git
git push -u origin master
```

Step 4: Deploy to Netlify

1. Sign up or log in to Netlify.

2. Click **"New Site from Git"** and choose **GitHub** as the repository source.

3. Select your repository (`my-app`).

4. **Build Settings**: Since this is a static site, no build commands are needed. Just select **Deploy Site**.

5. **Site URL**: After the deployment process, Netlify will provide a live URL (e.g., `https://my-app.netlify.app`).

Step 5: Check Your App

Open the provided URL to see your app live!

Conclusion

In this chapter, we:

- Discussed the **preparation process for deploying your JavaScript app**, including optimizing the code, using environment variables, and securing your app.

- Explored how to deploy apps on **Netlify**, **Heroku**, and **Vercel**, and the key differences between these platforms.

- Walked through a **real-world example** of deploying a simple **static web app** on **Netlify**.

Deploying your app is the final step in the development process. By choosing the right hosting platform and preparing your app for production, you ensure that it performs well and is secure for end users. In the next chapter, we will explore how to maintain and scale your applications after deployment.

CHAPTER 25

PROGRESSIVE WEB APPS (PWAS)

Progressive Web Apps (PWAs) represent a significant shift in how web applications are built, delivering app-like experiences on the web while leveraging the power of modern web technologies. PWAs combine the best features of both websites and mobile applications, providing fast, reliable, and engaging experiences for users.

In this chapter, we will:

- Explore what **Progressive Web Apps (PWAs)** are, along with their **key features**.
- Dive into **service workers** and their role in enabling **offline capabilities**.
- Walk through a **real-world example** of building a PWA with offline functionality.

What are Progressive Web Apps? Key Features of PWAs

A **Progressive Web App (PWA)** is a type of web application that uses modern web technologies to provide a native app-like experience on the web. PWAs are designed to work seamlessly across different devices, including desktops and mobile devices, without needing to be downloaded or installed through app stores.

Key Features of PWAs:

1. **Responsive**: PWAs are responsive and work across a wide range of devices, whether it's a mobile phone, tablet, or desktop computer.

2. **Offline Capability**: PWAs can work offline or in low-network conditions by caching important assets and data. This is achieved using **service workers** that enable background functionality even when the user is not connected to the internet.

3. **App-like Experience**: PWAs provide an app-like experience, offering smooth animations, fast interactions, and an intuitive user interface, just like native mobile apps.

4. **Installation on Home Screen**: PWAs can be installed directly to the user's device from the browser, bypassing app stores. They can be added to the home screen and launched like native apps.

5. **Push Notifications**: PWAs can send push notifications to users, enabling them to stay engaged with the app even when it's not open.

6. **Secure**: PWAs are served over **HTTPS**, ensuring that all data exchanged is secure and encrypted.

7. **Linkable**: Since PWAs are still web apps, they are accessible via URLs, making it easy to share and link to specific content.

Service Workers and Offline Capabilities

A **service worker** is a script that runs in the background of your browser, separate from your web page. Service workers allow you to manage how the app handles network requests, cache assets, and even serve cached content when the user is offline.

How Service Workers Work:

1. **Intercept Network Requests**: Service workers can intercept and manage network requests made by the app, allowing you to decide whether to fetch data from the network or serve it from the cache.
2. **Caching Assets**: Service workers can cache assets like images, CSS, JavaScript, and HTML files, so the app can function without an internet connection.
3. **Background Sync**: Service workers allow for background synchronization, meaning data can be stored and synced with the server when the network is available again.

Service Worker Lifecycle:

- **Registration**: The service worker script is registered in the main JavaScript file of the web app.
- **Installation**: When a service worker is installed, it caches assets for offline use.
- **Activation**: After installation, the service worker takes control of the page, enabling offline functionality.
- **Fetch**: The service worker intercepts network requests and can return cached assets or fetch new data from the network.

Service Worker Example:

javascript

```
// Registering the Service Worker
if ('serviceWorker' in navigator) {
    window.addEventListener('load', () => {

navigator.serviceWorker.register('/service-
worker.js').then(registration => {
            console.log('Service         Worker
registered with scope:', registration.scope);
        }).catch(error => {
            console.log('Service         Worker
registration failed:', error);
        });
    });
```

```
}
```

Offline Caching with Service Workers

In the service worker, we can specify which assets to cache and
how to handle fetch requests.

```javascript
// service-worker.js
const CACHE_NAME = 'my-pwa-cache-v1';
const urlsToCache = [
    '/',
    '/index.html',
    '/style.css',
    '/script.js',
];

// Install the service worker and cache assets
self.addEventListener('install', (event) => {
    event.waitUntil(
        caches.open(CACHE_NAME)
            .then((cache) => {
                return
cache.addAll(urlsToCache);
            })
    );
});

// Fetch event: serve cached content if offline
```

```
self.addEventListener('fetch', (event) => {
    event.respondWith(
        caches.match(event.request)
            .then((cachedResponse) => {
                // Return cached response if
found, otherwise fetch from network
                return         cachedResponse        ||
fetch(event.request);
            })
    );
});

// Activate the service worker and delete old
caches
self.addEventListener('activate', (event) => {
    const cacheWhitelist = [CACHE_NAME];
    event.waitUntil(
        caches.keys().then((cacheNames) => {
            return Promise.all(
                cacheNames.map((cacheName) => {
                    if
(!cacheWhitelist.includes(cacheName)) {
                        return
caches.delete(cacheName);
                    }
                })
            );
        })
    );
```

```
});
```

In this example:

- We register the service worker, and during installation, it caches a list of essential files (`index.html`, `style.css`, `script.js`).
- In the `fetch` event, we first try to serve the cached assets, and if they're not available, we fetch them from the network.
- The `activate` event ensures that old caches are cleaned up when the service worker is updated.

Real-World Example: Building a PWA with Offline Functionality

Now that we understand how to work with service workers, let's build a simple **PWA** that works offline.

Step 1: Create a Basic HTML/CSS/JavaScript App

Create a basic **index.html** with some content and a simple service worker registration.

index.html:

```
html
```

```
<!DOCTYPE html>
```

```html
<html lang="en">
<head>
    <meta charset="UTF-8">
    <meta name="viewport" content="width=device-
width, initial-scale=1.0">
    <title>PWA Offline Example</title>
    <link rel="stylesheet" href="style.css">
</head>
<body>
    <h1>Welcome to My PWA</h1>
    <p>This is a simple Progressive Web App that
works offline!</p>

    <script src="script.js"></script>
</body>
</html>
```

style.css:

css

```css
body {
    font-family: Arial, sans-serif;
    text-align: center;
    padding: 20px;
}

h1 {
    color: #333;
}
```

script.js:

```javascript
// Check if the browser supports service workers
if ('serviceWorker' in navigator) {
    window.addEventListener('load', () => {

navigator.serviceWorker.register('/service-worker.js')
            .then((registration) => {
            console.log('Service        Worker
registered with scope:', registration.scope);
            })
            .catch((error) => {
            console.log('Service        Worker
registration failed:', error);
            });
    });
}
```

Step 2: Create the Service Worker for Offline Functionality

Next, create a `service-worker.js` file to cache the assets and serve them offline.

service-worker.js:

```javascript
```

```
const CACHE_NAME = 'my-pwa-cache-v1';
const urlsToCache = [
    '/',
    '/index.html',
    '/style.css',
    '/script.js',
];


// Install the service worker and cache assets
self.addEventListener('install', (event) => {
    event.waitUntil(
        caches.open(CACHE_NAME)
            .then((cache) => {
                return
cache.addAll(urlsToCache);
            })
    );
});


// Fetch event: serve cached content if offline
self.addEventListener('fetch', (event) => {
    event.respondWith(
        caches.match(event.request)
            .then((cachedResponse) => {
                return     cachedResponse     ||
fetch(event.request);
            })
    );
});
```

Step 3: Testing the PWA

To test the PWA:

1. **Serve your app locally**: Use a local server (such as `http-server` or `Live Server` in VSCode) to serve the files.

2. **Enable Service Workers**: Open the browser's **Developer Tools** and make sure that service workers are active (check under the **Application** tab in Chrome DevTools).

3. **Test Offline**: Once the app is loaded, turn off your internet connection and try to reload the app. The app should still work, loading content from the cache.

Conclusion

In this chapter, we:

- Learned about **Progressive Web Apps (PWAs)**, including their key features like **offline capabilities, push notifications**, and **installability**.

- Explored how **service workers** enable offline functionality by caching assets and intercepting network requests.

- Built a **simple PWA** that works offline by caching essential assets and serving them when the network is unavailable.

PWAs are an exciting way to build fast, reliable, and engaging web apps. By incorporating service workers and other modern web features, you can provide users with a seamless experience, whether they are online or offline. In the next chapter, we will look at how to **optimize PWAs** further and integrate advanced features such as **background sync** and **push notifications**.

CHAPTER 26

NEXT STEPS: BECOMING A FULL-STACK DEVELOPER

Becoming a **full-stack developer** means mastering both the **frontend** (client-side) and **backend** (server-side) of web development. Full-stack developers are versatile, capable of handling both aspects of web applications and making architectural decisions on how they interact. This chapter will give you an overview of **full-stack development**, introduce **Node.js** and **Express.js** for backend development, and provide a **real-world example** of building a **full-stack app** using **React** and **Node.js**.

Overview of Full-Stack Development

Full-stack development refers to working on both the **frontend** (the user interface and client-side logic) and **backend** (the server, database, and application logic) of a web application. Full-stack developers are proficient in the entire web development stack, which typically includes:

- **Frontend**:

- o HTML, CSS, and JavaScript (React, Angular, Vue)
- o Design and user experience (UX/UI)
- o Handling user interactions with the application
- **Backend**:
  - o Server-side languages (JavaScript with Node.js, Python, Ruby, etc.)
  - o Server-side frameworks (Express.js, Django, etc.)
  - o Databases (SQL or NoSQL databases like MySQL, MongoDB)
  - o APIs and authentication
- **DevOps and Deployment**:
  - o Deployment platforms like **Heroku**, **Netlify**, or **Vercel**
  - o Continuous Integration (CI) and Continuous Deployment (CD)
  - o Server management, cloud hosting (AWS, DigitalOcean)

A full-stack developer works across the **entire stack**, from the client-side to the server-side, and is able to integrate all parts of the application.

301

Introduction to Node.js and Express.js for Backend Development

1. Node.js: JavaScript on the Server

Node.js is a JavaScript runtime built on Chrome's **V8 JavaScript engine** that allows developers to run JavaScript on the **server-side**. Unlike traditional server-side languages, Node.js uses JavaScript, making it possible to use the same language for both the **frontend** and **backend**.

Benefits of Node.js:

- **Non-blocking I/O**: Node.js is built on an event-driven, non-blocking I/O model, making it ideal for building scalable network applications.
- **Single Language Stack**: With Node.js, developers can write both frontend and backend code in JavaScript, simplifying the development process.
- **Large Ecosystem**: Node.js has a vast number of packages available through **npm** (Node Package Manager), making it easier to build and scale applications.

2. Express.js: A Minimalist Web Framework for Node.js

Express.js is a fast, minimal, and flexible Node.js web application framework that simplifies the process of building web applications and APIs. It provides tools for handling HTTP requests, routing, middleware integration, and more.

Key Features of Express.js:

- **Routing**: Handle different HTTP requests (GET, POST, PUT, DELETE) for various routes.
- **Middleware**: Easily manage requests and responses before they reach the final route handler.
- **Template Engines**: Render dynamic content in views.
- **Integration**: Easily integrates with databases, authentication libraries, and other middleware.

Real-World Example: Building a Full-Stack App using React and Node.js

Let's walk through the steps to build a simple **full-stack application** using **React** (for the frontend) and **Node.js with Express.js** (for the backend). The app will be a **simple blog**, where users can create and display blog posts.

Step 1: Setting Up the Backend with Node.js and Express.js

1. **Initialize the Project**: First, initialize the backend project with Node.js.

   bash

   ```
   mkdir backend
   cd backend
   ```

```bash
npm init -y
```

2. **Install Dependencies**: Install the necessary packages for backend development:

```
bash
```

```bash
npm install express mongoose cors
```

3. **Create the Express Server**: Create a `server.js` file to set up the Express server.

```
javascript
```

```javascript
const express = require('express');
const mongoose = require('mongoose');
const cors = require('cors');
const app = express();

app.use(cors());
app.use(express.json());

// Connect to MongoDB
mongoose.connect('mongodb://localhost:270
17/blogdb', {
    useNewUrlParser: true,
    useUnifiedTopology: true
});

// Define a Blog Post model
```

304

```javascript
const                BlogPost              =
mongoose.model('BlogPost', {
    title: String,
    content: String,
    author: String,
    datePosted: { type: Date, default:
Date.now }
});

// API to get all blog posts
app.get('/api/posts', async (req, res) =>
{
    const posts = await BlogPost.find();
    res.json(posts);
});

// API to create a new blog post
app.post('/api/posts', async (req, res) =>
{
    const { title, content, author } =
req.body;
    const newPost = new BlogPost({ title,
content, author });
    await newPost.save();
    res.json(newPost);
});

// Start the server
app.listen(5000, () => {
```

```
      console.log('Server    is    running    on
http://localhost:5000');
});
```

4. **Test the API**:

   o   Start the backend server with `node server.js`.

   o   Use **Postman** or **Insomnia** to test the API by sending GET and POST requests to `http://localhost:5000/api/posts`.

Step 2: Setting Up the Frontend with React

1. **Create a New React Project**: Open a new terminal and run the following commands to set up the frontend with React.

   `bash`

   ```
   npx create-react-app frontend
   cd frontend
   ```

2. **Install Axios for API Requests**: Install `axios` to make HTTP requests from the frontend to the backend.

   `bash`

   ```
   npm install axios
   ```

3. **Create the React Components**: In the `src` folder, create the following components:

App.js:

```javascript

import React, { useState, useEffect } from 'react';
import axios from 'axios';

function App() {
    const      [posts,      setPosts]      =
useState([]);
    const     [newPost,     setNewPost]     =
useState({ title: '', content: '', author:
'' });

    // Fetch posts from the backend API
    useEffect(() => {

axios.get('http://localhost:5000/api/post
s')
            .then(response               =>
setPosts(response.data))
            .catch(error                 =>
console.log(error));
    }, []);
```

```
// Handle form input changes
const handleChange = (e) => {
    const { name, value } = e.target;
    setNewPost({ ...newPost, [name]:
value });
};


// Submit new post to backend
const handleSubmit = (e) => {
    e.preventDefault();

axios.post('http://localhost:5000/api/pos
ts', newPost)
        .then(response => {
            setPosts([...posts,
response.data]);
            setNewPost({ title: '',
content: '', author: '' });
        })
        .catch(error                =>
console.log(error));
};


return (
    <div>
        <h1>My Blog</h1>
        <form onSubmit={handleSubmit}>
            <input
                type="text"
```

```
                        name="title"
                        placeholder="Title"
                        value={newPost.title}

onChange={handleChange}
                /> 
                <textarea
                        name="content"
                        placeholder="Content"

value={newPost.content}

onChange={handleChange}
                /> 
                <input
                        type="text"
                        name="author"
                        placeholder="Author"

value={newPost.author}

onChange={handleChange}
                /> 
                <button
type="submit">Create Post</button>
        </form>

        <h2>Blog Posts</h2>
        <ul>
```

```
{posts.map(post => (
    <li key={post._id}>

<h3>{post.title}</h3>

<p>{post.content}</p>
        <small>By
{post.author}</small>
        </li>
    ))}
    </ul>
  </div>
  );
}

export default App;
```

4. **Start the Frontend**: Run the React app:

```bash

npm start
```

5. **Connect Frontend and Backend**:
   - Make sure both the backend and frontend servers are running.
   - The React app will communicate with the Express API to fetch and display blog posts and create new ones.

Conclusion: Building a Full-Stack App

In this chapter, we:

- Explored the concept of **full-stack development** and the roles of frontend and backend in web applications.
- Learned about **Node.js** and **Express.js** for building backend APIs and interacting with databases.
- Built a simple **full-stack blog app** with **React** (frontend) and **Node.js with Express** (backend).

As a full-stack developer, you'll be able to handle both the frontend and backend of applications, enabling you to build fully integrated web applications. In the next chapter, we will dive deeper into **deploying** full-stack applications and integrating advanced features for scalability and performance.